# ARCHITECTURAL PRESENTATION TECHNIQUES

William Wilson Atkin

VNR VAN NOSTRAND REINHOLD COMPANY
New York  Cincinnati  London  Toronto  Melbourne

## Acknowledgments

This book would not be possible without the cooperation of all the architects, renderers, and photographers whose work appears herein. Often, priceless drawings were loaned so that the best possible reproduction could be obtained. I also want to thank Gino Misciagna, who contributed the series of drawings on composition in chapter 5 and who was helpful in many other ways. Douglas Miner contributed much technical help and comfort. Richard Bergmann let me use his studio for some photographs and provided helpful insights on the problems faced by architects in making up presentations. Thomas Larson, several of whose extraordinary renderings are included, gave solid and helpful advice, as did Herbert Gute, who teaches both painting and rendering at Yale. Jack Horner of Pennyroyal Productions was especially helpful in sharing some of his vast technical knowledge of photography. I owe gratitude to Dr. Peter Will and Arthur Appel of the Thomas B. Watson Research Center for their help in making computer graphics comprehensible to me and, I hope, to the reader. Finally, I want everyone to know that I particularly appreciate the help I got from my wife, Marilyn, who has an unerring eye for things beautiful.

Printed in the United States of America
Designed by Loudan Enterprises

Published in 1976 by Van Nostrand Reinhold Company
A Division of Litton Educational Publishing, Inc.
450 West 33rd Street
New York, NY 10001

Van Nostrand Reinhold Limited
1410 Birchmount Road
Scarborough, Ontario M1P 2E7, Canada

Van Nostrand Reinhold Australia Pty. Ltd.
17 Queen Street
Mitcham, Victoria 3132, Australia

Library of Congress Cataloging in Publication Data

Atkin, William Wilson.
    Architectural presentation techniques.

    Bibliography: p. 194
    Includes index.
    1. Architectural rendering.   2. Architectural
drawing.   3. Photography, Architectural.   4. Computer
drawing.   5. Architectural models.   I. Title.
NA2780.A84        720'.28        73-16697
ISBN 0-442-20361-6
7 6 5 4 3 2

# CONTENTS

# INTRODUCTION

In this book I have included presentations made by the designer himself, by members of a design team, and by independent outside renderers and photographers. While there are good arguments for the presentation to be made by the designer himself, there are often good reasons for having it done by some other individual or even by a team. The differences, in this writer's opinion, *can* be imperceptible providing the outside renderer really understands the building.

Architect Maynard Lyndon feels rather strongly that architects need to get back to simpler presentations, and those in this book fall, for the most part, in that category. Here are Mr. Lyndon's remarks:

> There seems to be an exaggerated idea of what presentation drawings must be like. We have seen so many instances recently, which *over*-presented, it became a reflection on the profession. Architects seem to delight in having elaborate and perfectly drawn documents to make their case. The technique becomes so professional it is confusing to the layman. Certainly the ultimate is to present a pleasant and descriptive image in the fewest possible lines, much as a good Picasso or Rembrandt line drawing. Perhaps elaboration suggests a lack of confidence in the concept of the design—or have architects let themselves be intimidated by excesses of competitors or by advertising techniques?

I have thought long and hard about the best way to present an architectural project and have concluded that generally a drawing or a combination of drawing and photography is superior to the model. There are many who will disagree with this conclusion. The model, like a building, is three-dimensional, but it is somewhat more difficult for the client to transmogrify himself from 5 to 6 feet to 1 or 1¼ inches or less. There is no need to do that in the case of a drawing or photograph, and, of course, the three dimensions read just as well. The great advantage of the model is that it may be viewed from all angles. In fact, photographs of an accurate model, particularly interior shots, are sometimes impossible to distinguish from the real thing. Another great advantage of drawing and photography over models is their relatively lower cost. In these days when time seems always to be pressing in on us, the rendering or photograph also can be completed much more quickly. For all these reasons, models appear in this book only as a means to an end. In addition, the subject of model making is much too vast to delve into here, and Sanford Hohauser's book, *Architectural and Interior Models*, is so definitive that it will be decades before anything new is needed.

In the creating of perspective, the most intriguing prospect is the omnipresent computer—the greatest love/hate symbol since the automobile. The potential it represents is explored in chapter 10 through the kindness of Prof. Raniero Corbelletti and Prof. Ray Masters, both of the School of Architecture, Pennsylvania State University.

To summarize, I have attempted to do several things at the same time in this book:

1. Include examples of pencil renderings from the simplest fine or heavy line drawings to examples of pencil pictures.

2. Include examples of work ranging from in-house sketches to finished renderings in pencil and in various ink and watercolor techniques as well as combinations of all kinds. Where appropriate, the work is reproduced in color.

3. Explore and explain the various techniques employed in 1 and 2.

4. Describe simple and complex methods of presentation using a camera and projector in combination with sketching, or with models, plot plans, and other materials and activities.

5. Examine the use of computers in turning out perspectives.

The material in this book is intended not only for architectural offices but for students of architecture. It is my hope that it will prove useful.

# 1. PENCIL RENDERINGS

Until computer magic makes it possible to turn out all contract documents on verbal command without paper, drawing instruments of any kind, or a typewriter for specifications—a not unlikely development—the architect will continue to think with a pencil, to sketch plans, perspectives, elevations, sections, and details free-hand. Yet the development and improvement of India ink fine line and felt or nylon-tip fountain pens, magic markers, and ball-point pens make ink sketching as easy, often easier, than pencil. Color coding, highlights, tones and shadows may be executed more simply with colored pens than with pastels or colored pencils.

In view of all this, it seems incredible that anything new could be produced in the way of pencil rendering, yet changing styles in architecture demand changing rendering techniques. The changes that have occurred are probably rediscoveries of "lost" styles, of course. The pencil picture holds its own along with fine line, broad stroke, and combination pencil techniques. But new mixed media techniques are possible, cheap, and easy since the development of various reprographic processes—diazo, office copiers, cameras, and their accompanying films and papers. It is not at all unusual—though it was in 1953, when Raniero Corbelletti, Vincent Fiore, and I collaborated on *Pencil Tech-niques in Modern Design*—for an architect to make a drawing in pencil or pen and ink, reproduce it mechanically, add dashes of color, and send what looks like original drawings to boards of clients all over the country or the world.

In 1565, upon the discovery of the first important graphite mine in Borrowdale, England, a rough approximation of the pencil, as we know it today, appeared. Because this lode was so pure, the graphite from it could be sawed into thin sheets, then resawed into strips and glued into wood cases for protection in use. The British would not permit the export of Borrowdale graphite except in the form of finished wood-encased pencils, which became known in Europe as "*crayons d'Angleterre.*" Like many natural resources, graphite proved useful to the military, so by 1678 the highest quality graphite in this limited lode was exhausted. Early in the eighteenth century however, a new, even richer lode was discovered in Borrowdale, but by the end of the century, this lode, too, was used up.

More or less successful attempts at making graphite pencils with much lower-quality graphite than that available at Borrowdale were in progress. The problem was to find binders suitable for use with pulverized graphite, and pencils were being made, by hand, with great difficulty and at great expense early in the eighteenth century.

Kaspar Faber was one of the pioneer pencil manufacturers; his business was founded near Nuremberg, Germany, in 1761. Nicholas Jacques Conté, a French mechanic and chemist, discovered, in 1790, a process of combining pulverized graphite with clay and water to form a paste from which, by an involved process, pencils could be manufactured in quantity. This discovery was made contemporaneously in Vienna by Josep Hardtmuth, who founded the L. & C. Hardtmuth Company. Conté and Hardtmuth immediately began to produce pencils by the new method. The Dixon Crucible Company in the United States began manufacturing pencils in 1820, but had trouble selling them because people still preferred to cut their own quills and write with ink. It was not until the Civil War, when soldiers in the field wished to write home, that pencil sales built up to a respectable volume.

Pencil. Pier 88, New York, New York. Warren Platner Associates Architects.

Isobel Roberts House. Joseph F. Hennessy, renderer. Frank LLoyd Wright, architect.

The terms used to describe drawing and writing materials would be an interesting line of inquiry. Crayon, the French word for pencil, apparently referred to chalk at first. At least one would gather that this was so, because on discovery of the Borrowdale lode the resulting writing implement was called a *crayon noire*. Graphite, when first discovered, was called "black lead," which explains the term "lead" pencil. However, during the Middle Ages the term "pencil" was used to refer to a very small brush used by artists; this connotation is still current in some quarters. Besides graphite, silver, copper, and gold were shaped into drawing instruments. The parchment and paper on which these were used was coated with various animal and mineral matter ground and suspended in an aqueous gluelike medium, and lines drawn with the stylus left fine particles of the metal on the paper. The lines were pale gray and in time corroded to a slightly darker value and warmer tone. Apparently these instruments were known collectively as silverpoint, though some were of the mineral lead or a combination of lead and tin.

Graphite pencils must have been used as early as the sixteenth century, although who first used them for writing or drawing, and where, is difficult to know. The confusion with the mineral lead adds to the difficulty. It was not until the eighteenth century that anything like the graphite pencil, so omnipresent today, was regularly used.

Crayons, composed of pigment in an oil or wax, were used much earlier in Europe. Chalk was known and used for drawing from the earliest times. Leonardo da Vinci has been credited with the first complete drawing in chalk. During his period, chalk was found as a natural deposit in the earth and was usually black or red, although white chalk was also known and used by artists. Charcoal, another ancient drawing medium, was known and used widely. The charcoal produced by burning willow twigs was highly favored, but an altered form of charcoal was used in the seventeenth century, when charcoal was treated by dipping and cooking it in linseed oil.

The renderings included here were chosen to show the range of today's pencil techniques.

Ink and pencil on tracing paper. Competition design for Architectural Association Building in London, England. Martin Holub, architect and renderer.

**Renderer:** Bob Perry: Perry and Gravois
**Architects:** Curtis and Davis and Associated Architects Inc.; Edward B. Silverstein and Associates, Architects, Inc.; Nolan, Norman, and Nolan, Architects; Sverdrup & Parcel and Associates, Inc.
**Louisiana Stadium Project** New Orleans, Louisiana

This very realistic pencil rendering was executed 30″ × 40″ on medium gray board, in medium rough texture with graphite pencils. Curtis and Davis says that their normal preference is for renderings to be executed in the office by the natural techniques architects learn in school. However, since the client often prefers the more commercial tempera watercolor rendering, the firm uses both approaches.

**Renderer:** David Winfield Scott
**Architect:** David Winfield Scott
**Residence** Great Exuma, Bahamas

These two renderings, each of which was traced over a mechanically constructed perspective, took Mr. Scott about two or three hours to draw. The originals are 8″ × 10″ on vellum.

**Renderer:** Patrick Lopez
**Architects:** Skidmore, Owings and Merrill
**Fourth Financial Corporation** Wichita, Kansas

An ebony pencil, of the softest grade, approximately 6B, was used for both of these renderings. They are part of a set of four drawings the renderer completed in about five days. The originals were on illustration board: the exterior approximately 24″ × 33″, the interior 24″ × 27″. Mr. Lopez likes the pencil because it is so much less formal than pen and ink. These renderings were executed for presentation to the client and were prepared from a constructed perspective. However, when models are available, the renderer uses photographs of these to establish his vanishing points. Mr. Lopez admires the renderings of the Viennese architect, Otto Wagner, and of Helmut Jacoby, to whom he feels indebted because he believes his own style developed from these sources. It is his feelings that renderings should reflect the personality of the artist who produces them as well as the architecture they portray. All figures and other entourage in Mr. Lopez's renderings are drawn by his hand.

He says that the poorer the architecture, the more need for slickness in presentation. For that reason, for a well-designed building like this one he feels the pencil is the logical drawing instrument. However, Skidmore, Owings and Merrill often ask for pen and ink or combination techniques; examples of Mr. Lopez's work in this medium are shown on pages 68 and 69.

**Renderer:** Raniero Corbelletti
**Architects:** Hood & Fouilhoux
**Original McGraw-Hill Building** New York

On cold-pressed illustration board, 20″ × 30″, this rendering was especially executed to demonstrate the scumbling technique.

It is easy to see how the renderer blocked in the building and its surroundings and then executed tones by using his pencils in a circular motion, except for a few areas where this was not appropriate. The lighter and medium tones were executed with a relatively hard pencil (3H) while the darkest tones were done with a B pencil. It took approximately four hours to complete this rendering.

**Renderer:** Stanley J. Trela
**Engineers and builders:** The Austin Company
**Proposed Office Building**

Drawn on rag bond tracing paper, 18″ × 26″, with F, B, and 2B pencils, this rendering started with perspective charts constructed by the renderer. Mr. Trela describes the steps he followed to complete the rendering:

1. Over the chart I placed a sheet of tracing paper, penciling in line the proposed building. Using actual site photos as reference, I laid out the surrounding buildings and added the entourage.

2. On a sheet of rag bond tracing paper, with a good "tooth," I followed with details, using the F pencil for outlines, B and 2B for shade and shadows. The dark glass areas were put in with B pencil strokes and blended smooth with a gray paper stump.

3. Over a print of the above completed rendering I placed another sheet of smooth tracing paper and with an Exacto knife cut out areas I wanted to remain light. Areas that were to be toned down were left intact, thereby creating a mask. This mask was placed over the original finished pencil rendering, and wherever darker areas were wanted, additional cut-outs were placed on top of the mask for the desired effect. All cut-outs were held in place with spots of rubber cement.

4. A black and white print was made from the masked drawing. Fresh stock black line paper was used and extreme care was taken as to proper speed of printing and the dilution of the ammonia wash.

By employing the value system as he did, the renderer brings the eye directly to his own building despite the fact that buildings on both sides were much taller and more voluminous. The detailing of the automobiles adds to the realism of the drawing. Though the drawing is excellent full size for display, when reduced down to size in a newspaper or magazine, it clearly imparts its message. The heaviness of line also makes this drawing excellent for shooting down to 35mm. slide size.

**Renderer:** Ralph Rapson
**Architects:** Ralph Rapson and Van der Meulen
**United States Embassy Office Building** The Hague, Holland

Rendered in pencil on tracing paper, this drawing was used as a study in-house and for publicity. The building, designed in 1951, will probably not be realized because the project was assigned to another architect.

The architects say the building was "a difficult and interesting assignment. The site was on an old and lovely square whose buildings were small in scale and traditional in character. The architects attempted to recognize these factors by maintaining overall heights, sympathetic materials, and a 'dissolved' facade that would harmonize with the older buildings."

Knowing what the architects wished to accomplish, it is easy to see how well Mr. Rapson's drawing technique conveyed those wishes.

**Renderer:** Ralph Rapson
**Architects:** Ralph Rapson and Associates, Inc.
**St. Paul Arts and Science Center** St. Paul,
Minnesota

This one-point perspective was executed in various weights of graphite pencil on tracing paper, 30″ × 40″. Yellow Prismacolor was added on the back of a print of this rendering on tracing paper as a sky background. It was then used for publicity purposes.

**Renderer:** F. Nemeth
**Architect:** Ralph Rapson and Associates, Inc.
**International Studies Building** University of Chicago, Chicago, Illinois

This drawing was done in pencil on tracing paper, 29" × 30". It is interesting to compare the way entourage is handled by Mr. Rapson (page 15), Mr. Nemeth, and Mr. Gebhart in the next drawing. For example, in this drawing trees are realistic while Mr. Gebhart's trees are quite stylized.

**Renderer:** Mike Gebhart
**Architect:** Ralph Rapson and Associates
**Performing Arts Building** University of Minnesota,
Minneapolis, Minnesota

Mr. Gebhart's drawing was rendered in various
grades of graphite pencil on tracing paper, 30″ ×
40″, over an in-house perspective Mr. Rapson had
done earlier. It was used for publicity.

**Renderer:** Jay Henderson Barr
**Architects:** Warren Platner Associates for **Mortgage Guarantee Investment Corporation Headquarters;** Skidmore, Owings & Merrill for **MGIC Plaza**

The drawing was executed in pencil on Mylar, 10″ × 13″. The detail (in which his original 10″ × 13″ rendering was blown up to photo-mural size) shows how Mr. Barr achieved his various effects on this ultra-smooth medium. The full photo would make a mural 18½″ × 24″.

**Renderer:** Jay Henderson Barr
**Architect:** Warren Platner Associates
**Teknor-Apex Company** Pawtucket, Rhode Island

Executed in pencil on Mylar, 10″ × 15″, this drawing is particularly interesting because of the way the mirror wall, to the left, is rendered. As with all of his drawings, Mr. Barr constructs a perspective adjusted to look correct. Every stroke of the pencil is rendered individually with a carbon pencil or sepia Prismacolor. Mr. Barr's aim is to produce drawings with presence and style which, nevertheless, show the subject with realism rather than abstracted.

**Renderer:** Martin Holub
**Architect:** David Kenneth Specter
**Project Designer:** Martin Holub
**Setauket Center Housing Development** Setauket,
Long Island, New York

A fine-line rendering in pencil on Mylar, 20″ ×
30″, this drawing was used for client presentation
and publicity.

Mr. Holub feels a properly constructed perspective provides as true a representation of the shapes
and spaces of a design as a good photograph does
of the realized project. Since he uses perspectives
as a means of verifying design intentions, he is
careful in deciding on view points.

He says: "Architects who do not construct their
perspectives do not draw the shapes and spaces
they designed but those they think they designed.
That is why I don't believe in 'eye-balling' [drawing
perspectives by heart—from imagination].

"I believe a good architect himself draws perspectives of his designs. The whole profession of
'perspective artists' or 'professional renderers' is,
in my view, a sign of decay.

"I believe that perspectives, as all other architectural drawings, should be reproducible by conventional printing methods. Therefore, all my perspectives are drawn on tracing paper or Mylar in
ink or pencil or combination of both. If a client de-
sires a color representation, I color up prints in
watercolor or Prismacolor."

Another of Mr. Holub's drawings is reproduced
on page 97.

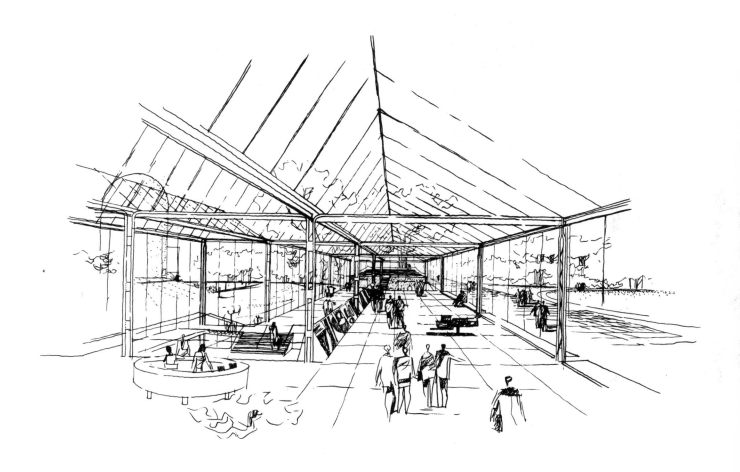

**Renderer:** Romaldo Guirgola
**Architects:** Mitchell/Guirgola Associates
**Con Edison—Indian Point Simulator—Visitors
Center**  Buchanan, New York

This is a fine-line schematic sketch rendered in pencil on Clearprint tracing vellum. The original is 30″ × 42″.

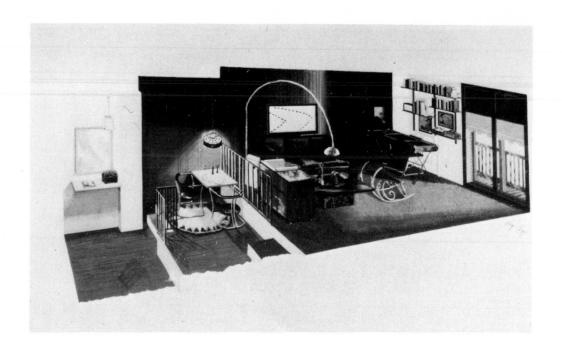

**Renderer:** Wayne Ruga
**Designer:** Wayne Ruga Interiors
**Studio Apartment Design** and Individual Pieces of Furniture

Mr. Ruga prefers to use the traditional approach of providing photographic realism in his renderings. This technique is rarely used today because its cost for small-scale jobs is prohibitive. The studio apartment drawing was 14″ × 26″ and the furniture drawing 20″ × 22″.

Here is Mr. Ruga's description of his method:

The original layouts were initially prepared as free-hand pencil sketches on vellum. Once a satisfactory sketch was obtained, vanishing points and a straight edge were used to firm up the composition. The vellum layout was then transferred via tracing tissue onto Bainbridge illustration board #80. Most of the colors were prepared at this point and the rendering began with the largest mass areas first. Color relationships were established during this phase. Work progressed from background to foreground. The opaque quality of the watercolor medium lends itself to this method and to the necessary modeling of forms. The perspective linead was used when extremely distant vanishing points were necessary but not feasible because of the limitations of drawing board lengths.

**Renderer:** Paul Thiry
**Architect:** Thiry Architects
**Libby Dam Project** Montana

The first two renderings were drawn with a Conté pencil. The third was drawn with a William Korn lithographic crayon, also known as a grease pencil. The line work was done with an Eagle Prismacolor because, Mr. Thiry says, it is reasonably sturdy and can be sharpened to a point. The lithographic crayon is good for tone quality. The perspectives were a combination of projection and eye which the architect finds reasonably accurate and fast. The originals were all approximately 15″ × 20″ and executed on Clearprint 1000 H tracing paper. One of tracing paper's advantages is that it is easy to correct the perspective on outlay. In addition, prints in sepia, brown, blue, or black are readily reproduced from the original, and the surface of tracing paper has good textural appeal when a Conté pencil or litho crayon is used.

Mr. Thiry makes these additional comments:

The use of large freely-drawn sketches are very valuable when presenting ideas to a client. They are equally useful in introduction to staff who will develop ideas into construction documents.

Techniques which require careful layout and drawing are primarily acceptable for final presentation, publication, etc., but the quick sketch will permit production of dozens of views while a single more accurate drawing is in production.

**Renderer:** Granville Ackermann
**Designers:** Facility Design Consultants Corporation
**Operator-Assisted Call Facility** New York Telephone Company, Grand Central Station, New York, N.Y.

The renderer, whose drawing is on page 25, and the photographer, whose work accompanies it, seem to have been in cahoots in deciding on viewpoint and distance from subject. The renderer did not construct a mechanical perspective but depended on his eye, plus familiarity with the plans and elevations, in making his drawing. Some eye! Except for minor changes made after the rendering was complete, the client knew exactly what to expect.

In executing the rendering, perspective and basic design were first roughed out on yellow Oriola sketch paper, approximately 18″ × 26″. The rough was then mounted to a toothy, pebble-finish white matte board. The final rendering, on a piece of transparent Oriola on top of the rough sketch, was then traced using charcoal sticks and charcoal pencils, and white chalk and Conté white pencils. The pebble matte finish of the board provides an even texture and imparts tooth to the otherwise smooth finish of the Oriola. Periodically, during applications of charcoal and chalk, the sketch was sprayed with fixative to prevent smearing. The only way a dense, solid black can be achieved is to build up the charcoal and spray fixative from time to time to increase density from gray to black. For the molding of tones from white to gray to black, the finger was used to smear the charcoal, but a paper stump might also have been used. The final application of chalk should not be sprayed because the fixative will destroy the absolutely pure white the chalk provides.

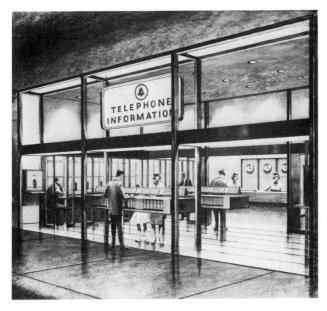

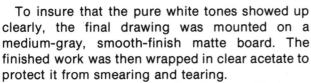

To insure that the pure white tones showed up clearly, the final drawing was mounted on a medium-gray, smooth-finish matte board. The finished work was then wrapped in clear acetate to protect it from smearing and tearing.

This technique is most effective in achieving a photographic appearance. It is also time-saving, requiring approximately 2½ to 3 hours from the beginning of the rough sketch to the completion of the rendering. Granville Ackermann says of his approach:

Facility Design Consultants of New York, feeling that not all members of a client group can "read" floor plans, elevations, sections, and reflected ceiling plans, takes the approach that a client should be fully informed about final design recommendations. Complete comprehension by the client of the eventual function and appearance of the project is more important than rendering technique or drafting styles. By going through a full exploration and disclosure, the designer also completes the design phase more thoroughly, helps eliminate client editorializing, and cost overruns, as well as those surprise problems that can crop up in the final phases of construction drawings.
Interior design, insofar as presentation is concerned, embodies a dimension of design and engineering that architects do not always have to deal with—artificial lighting. A building design can be presented in a perspective line drawing with no tone or shading whatsoever since natural daytime, ambient lighting is implied. In interior design, lighting is integral to the design and must be evident in

visualizations. A line sketch of an interior with no indication of the behavior of the lighting design does not show the complete design. Too much is left to the client's imagination. For only a professional, thoroughly experienced in lighting techniques, can imagine this ultimate appearance.

For these reasons, all Facility Design Consultants' renderings are executed in a full range of tones from black-darkness to white-light. Generally, unless inappropriate to the project, the renderings depict nighttime. Thus, all light sources are artificial and, therefore, indicative of the actual results.

To further simplify communications with the client, renderings are executed only in black and white. Actual samples of all materials recommended for the project are shown to permit close inspection for color, touch, and behavior under real conditions. Showing the total design in full-color renderings assumes that the client can absorb and comprehend everything at one time. Clients can think they dislike a design because of its color scheme without realizing that personal color preferences have interfered with their objectivity. Black and white renderings call attention to the subject of design and lighting, allowing the oftentimes controversial subject of color to be treated separately.

The rendering is reproduced twice—once as originally rendered and once cropped exactly as the photograph is cropped. Would the original rendering be more effective cropped to provide a solid ceiling line and to remove the bright sign and pedestrian movement on the left side?

**Renderer:** Jan Talbot
**Architects:** Caudill Rowlett Scott
**Howard Educational Park Project** Wilmington, Delaware

Quick perspectives, like this one-point pencil sketch, are used by Caudill Rowlett Scott for in-house design discussions. Sometimes, as in this case, solid or screen colored Zippatone masks are added and the same sketch can be used for discussions with the client.

Caudill Rowlett Scott says, however: "Our approach to architecture really does not require the use of renderings. We make wide use of such tools as study models and quick sketches (like this one), tools that provide maximum work-study benefit for the time spent. They are also an effective means of graphic communication with a client. We find that renderings, which provide a minimum working tool for time required, are not typically needed." When specifically asked by the client, the firm will have an outside delineator prepare a rendering.

**Renderer:** Robert Kaminski
**Architects:** Welton Becket and Associates
**Transpo 72,** Dulles International Airport
Washington, D.C.

Because this rendering was to show open space rather than buildings, it is particularly interesting for its entourage. Mr. Kaminski has provided a strong feeling of activity with his spanking flags, jet armada, figures, and vehicles, all of which look as though they were really moving. The lack of linear definition and the combination of vertical and diagonal strokes help accomplish this end; in fact, the only horizontal lines are those on the pole in front of the geodesic dome in the left background. The original, drawn on tracing paper with an Eagle drafting pencil, was 20″ × 30″. Another rendering of this project by Mr. Kaminski appears on page 65.

**Renderer:** Larry Perron
**Architects:** Marcel Breuer and Herbert Beckhard
**Community for Argentina, Brazil, Paraguay and Uruguay,** Interama, Miami, Florida 1965–1966

Quite the opposite of Mr. Kaminski's rendering, this bird's-eye view of a community features a complex of buildings. Nevertheless, the renderer has managed to bring his drawing to life by his use of miniscule figures throughout the project, and by his cunning use of sailboats at strategic places. The handling of boats by the renderer indicates he may be on familiar terms with them.

**Renderer:** Norman Jaffe
**Architect:** Norman Jaffe
**Perlbinder House** Sagoponak, New York

This rendering was executed on Mylar with Ebony pencil #6325 and Prismacolor #944. The texture obtained in this drawing and the next one comes from putting a piece of rough cardboard under the Mylar and from using the side of the pencil. A chamois was also used with the graphite pencil.

Two methods were employed to bring through pure whites. For small areas, an eraser with an erasing shield are used, and, for larger areas, holes were cut in the originals so that pure white would come through when printed on Mylar.

Mr. Jaffe has this to say about the importance of renderings vis-à-vis models:

Perspective renderings in any medium are most important in our work. It is true it's possible to deceive oneself by selecting the most advantageous points of view to develop the drawing from. At the same time, walking around the piece of work, vignetting as many conditions as possible, is most essential to developing a sense of the architecture. We have found that the younger people in our office are more inclined to rely on models. This is good too. However, we generally build a model only after we've completely "walked" the building inside and out with perspective studies. Ernest Born at Berkeley helped me realize the infinite excitement in the color of light through leaves, reflections, and the power of direct shadows. It is most helpful if the hand that delineates the building is connected to the mind that conceives it.

**Renderer:** Norman Jaffe
**Architect:** Norman Jaffe
**Shelter Mountain Inn**

This rendering was executed on Mylar 36″ × 24″
with three Prismacolor pencils: black, raw umber,
and burnt orange. Mr. Jaffee places a rough-
textured material under the ultra-smooth Mylar
to accomplish his textural effects. A color rendering of the three houses shown on the next page
appears on page 179, and five drawings appear on
pages 112 and 113.

**Renderer:** Norman Jaffe
**Architect:** Norman Jaffe
**Three Houses on Shelter Island** Off the North
Shore of Long Island in New York State

The original color rendering of these three houses
(here reproduced in black and white) was executed
on full-sheet watercolor paper, 22″ × 38″. The
renderer starts his work by laying in light washes
for the sky and foreground, having first masked out,
with liquid mask, the areas where the houses will

appear. He continues with transparent or acrylic
watercolor, working in the traditional light-to-dark
progression. When the watercolor is completely dry,
he draws in the houses, using black and raw sienna
Prismacolor pencils for the ruled lines. How faith-
fully the renderings depicted the finished houses
may be seen in the series of photographs shown
here.

In the illustration, the Seidler house is at left,
the Osofsky house is in the center, and the Jacobs
house is at right. Photos are by Bill Maris.

**Renderer:** Thomas Larson
**Architects:** Progressive Design Associates:
Thomas Larson, Peter Woytuk, Thomas Van
Housen, and Don Hansen
**Boston City Hall** Competition, Finalist Entry—1962

The renderer's dramatic use of a value rendering and realistic treatment of figures create interest.

The textured areas were executed with the grease pencil while the smooth delineation and solid areas were worked with the Prismacolor pencil on white vellum, 30″ × 40″. The excellent treatment of entourage in no way allows the eye to stray from the essential dramatic sweep of the building itself.

This is an example of a surprisingly complex one-point perspective drawing. PDA's entry into the Boston City Hall Competition, this rendering was prepared to be examined and judged chiefly by architects on the jury.

**Renderer:** Gino Misciagna
**Architect:** Le Corbusier
**Ronchamp Chapel** France

This drawing was executed on illustration board with a smooth finish, 15″ × 20″. The building was first blocked in and then tones were built up gradually using a 3B pencil. Notice especially the way the strokes are built up in the roof area to indicate clearly the sculptured curves. The only entourage consists of a tree to the right, some shurbs to the left, and the merest indications of grass in the foreground.

**Renderer:** Allen G. Siple
**Scottish War Memorial** Scotland

In six years as editor of the *Bulletin* of the Southern California Chapter of the American Institute of Architects, the late Allen G. Siple made it one of the liveliest and most interesting of all regional architectural magazines. Through the kindness of his widow, Josephine Siple, we have this example of his pencil drawing technique. In a tribute to him shortly before he retired, the Chapter addressed him as architect/editor/student of mankind. They might easily have added artist.

The Scottish War Memorial was one among a group of pencil drawings made by Mr. Siple, a dedicated Caledonian, on one of his visits to Scotland.

**Renderer:** Joseph F. Hennessy
**Architect:** Frank LLoyd Wright
**Robie House,** 5757 S. Woodlawn, Chicago, Illinois, 1908

The purpose of this rendering, according to Mr. Hennessy, was to advertise his rendering business. It is part of a set which was later combined into a calendar. The rendering was executed on 1000 H tracing paper, 12½" × 19". After completion it was wet mounted on illustration board. The graphite pencils employed were in grades H-2B-4B-6B.

A rendering by Mr. Hennessy in another medium will be found on page 81.

The Robie house, which was saved from the wrecker's ball through the intervention of realtor William Zeckendorf, then president of Webb & Knapp, has since become headquarters for the Adlai E. Stevenson Institute in Chicago. A rendering of the living room, which was restored by Skidmore, Owings and Merrill, appears on page 80. There is a rendering of the Isobel Roberts house by Mr. Hennessy on page 7.

# 2. HOW TO RENDER IN PENCIL

Just as a dentist or even the carpenter must be able to select the exact tool for a particular job, so must the artist be able to choose, automatically, the exact tool to achieve the effect he is after. He also must become master of his own vocabulary of lines, squiggles, strokes, dots, shades, and tones if he is to render successfully. The late great illustrator, Albert Dorne, once showed a movie that unfolded exactly how he produced his incredible drawings with colored ink for *Saturday Evening Post*, *Collier's* and other magazines. After it was over, a wag in the audience asked, "Aren't you afraid, Al, that you won't get any more work now that you've shown all your secrets?" "I'm not worried," Dorne wagged back, "because there's one important ability I have that most people do not have. I'm a hell of a good *drawerer*." Most of the architects and renderers whose works appear in these pages like to draw; many obviously would just as soon draw and paint all day as they would design buildings. The moral, of course, is that the student who becomes a good "drawerer" is the one who has practiced and practiced until the business of picking the right tone, the right stroke, and the right tool comes as naturally to him as picking the right note comes to a jazz musician improvising a composition.

## PAPER, CLOTH, BOARD AND FILM

Every renderer has his favorite surface on which to draw; most, naturally, choose a material to suit best the job at hand. Tracing paper seems to be the choice of most of the renderers whose work appears in this book. Everything from the cheapest yellow paper to the most expensive vellum is used by renderers, and with today's diazo methods, a pencil drawing on any grade of tracing paper, reproduced on transparent or opaque acetate or polyester film, will look better than the original. Boards of various kinds are usually used for presentation renderings, but tracing paper is dry mounted on board. A sheet with a slight "tooth" to it is most satisfactory for pencil or ink work, but boards with smooth surfaces and rough surfaces are also appropriate for some types of drawing. Tracing cloth can be used effectively for ink rendering but is not often so employed.

The new entrant into the field of drawing surfaces, which elicits great enthusiasm among renderers and architects who have used it, is film. Most of these drawing surfaces are coatings applied to a polyester film manufactured by du Pont and their licencees. Some of the coated films are acetate; nevertheless, for reasons unknown, the du Pont trade name for the raw polyester film—Mylar—has become almost a generic term applied to film drawing surfaces by most renderers, architects, and even art supply dealers. Suppliers and manufacturers of drafting materials who apply the various coatings refer to them by their own trade names or simply as acetate or polyester tracing film. Renderers usually prefer clear polyester-based film with an opaque coating, which will take a pencil, ink, color, or airbrush on one or both sides. Polyester-based material is tough, durable, and stable, whereas acetate will tear and become brittle with age. These films also are available treated with an absolutely transparent coating which will take wash or watercolor. Such film is useful when combining drawings with photographs.

Besides opaque and transparent, stock papers and film are available in a variety of colors, and some are sensitized to print lines in blue, green, pink, or yellow. Specialty papers and other materials of passing interest are a card stock in blue, cherry, or white which prints in black; plastic-coated sensitized paper which prints in black or blue; and a heavy white plastic-coated paper or high gloss continuous-tone paper which prints in black only.

Until recently film and photographic paper were considered the exclusive province of the photographer. But once an architect or renderer discovers what a magnificent material film can be to draw on, he is hooked. Photographic paper in conjunction with those old-fashioned paints that were used to "tint" black and white photography have also been found helpful.

Most paper, cloth, and films are available sensitized for dry or wet prints, and reflex film is available for copying from opaque materials. The equipment in most blueprint houses today is varied and while more complicated from an engineering point of view, it is much simpler from the point of view of operation. The familiar smell of ammonia is fast disappearing as odorless dry-copy machines replace their older counterparts.

Black, blue, or sepia line prints are made on opaque paper or on tracing paper, tracing cloth, or any of the various film products. Often, the sensitized lines can be erased and the surface can be drawn on in pencil, ink, or watercolor.

One thing to consider in specifying the new materials is that all of the line work is not stable; much of it will fade away after a time, especially if it is left in the light. However, some of the films are not only stable in themselves (the polyesters) but are tough and are sensitized to hold lines permanently under all conditions.

Paper test: 4B pencil on mylar, smooth board, medium board, and average tracing paper.

## GRAPHITE PENCILS

From the enormous range of pencils available, those traditionally associated with pencil rendering are graphite. These range from hardest (9H) to softest (6B) as follows: Hard pencils step down from 9H to H; in the center are F and HB; and grades B to 6B are on the soft end of the scale. Pencils from 10H to 8B, equally graded, are manufactured by Swan. If handed a 9H pencil, anyone unfamiliar with this range would be likely to call it a nail. Most renderers find the middle to soft range the most useful. Thus a beginner might need a 3H, an H, a B, and a 3B. A 6B might also be useful just to get the feel of a very soft graphite pencil.

Sketching pencils with round, oval, and flat leads also are available in various grades, as are layout pencils which have thick round leads. While many such pencils are often manufactured for use by students, they are available in various grades, and the flat ones in particular (with rectangular leads 3/16" × 3/8"), are useful for laying in tones in large areas. General has a line of such pencils graded like drawing pencils. Those made for school use are usually not of as high quality as fine drawing pencils and are available in fewer grades by name. Dixon, for example, calls their series, from hard to soft, Outline (2260), Drawing (2264), Rendering (2266), Deep Shading (2270), and Sketching (2275).

Dixon Crucible Company is most interested in producing pencils for draftsmen. As a result, they have been working with new graphite formulations and will phase out their famous El Dorado line in favor of a new series of graphite pencils in the traditional grades 9H to 6B to be known as DTR (for Drawing Tracing Reproductions).

Texture test on Mylar

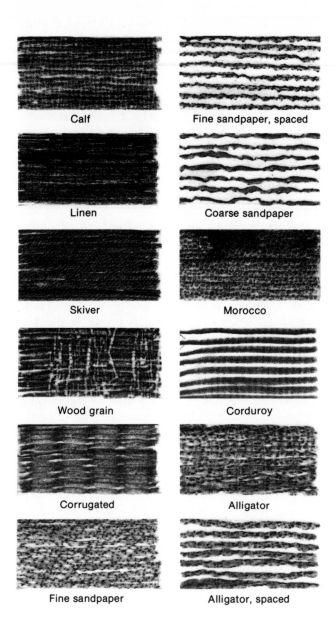

Calf

Fine sandpaper, spaced

Linen

Coarse sandpaper

Skiver

Morocco

Wood grain

Corduroy

Corrugated

Alligator

Fine sandpaper

Alligator, spaced

Some pencil grades on smooth board (left) and medium board (right).

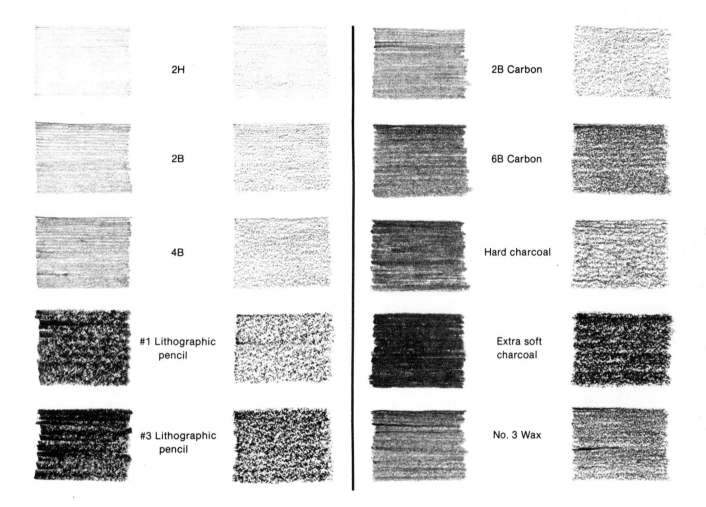

2H

2B

4B

#1 Lithographic
pencil

#3 Lithographic
pencil

2B Carbon

6B Carbon

Hard charcoal

Extra soft
charcoal

No. 3 Wax

Various applications of different grades are reproduced here on "average" paper the same size as they were drawn. The student should experiment with different makes and grades of pencils on different surfaces.

4B (#2)

4B (#1)

2B (#3)   Heavy to light

6B (#4)    Light to heavy

(#5) HB pencil

6H (#6)

41

Examples of 2B and 4B graphite sticks used for continuous tone
and for notched tone.

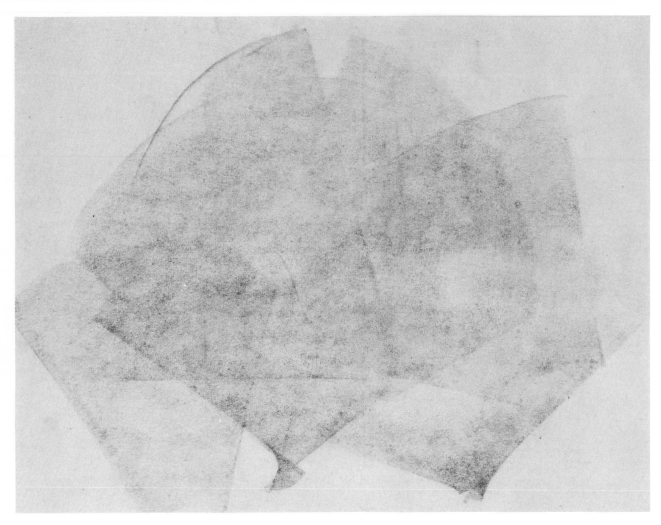

Graphite stick for toning

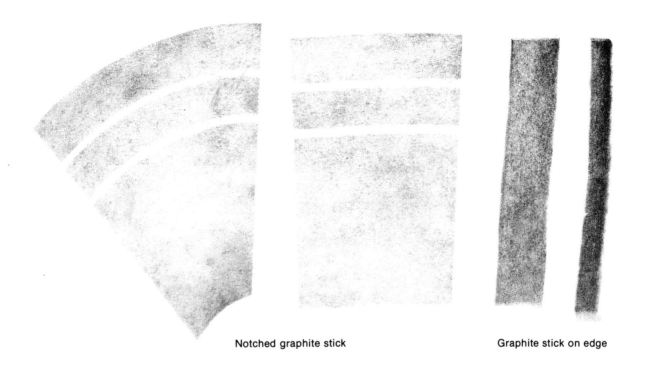

Notched graphite stick      Graphite stick on edge

Graphite stick on edge

Some experimental strokes are reproduced here same size. Some represent materials and textures, others are simply typical strokes for pencil work. Try these and then examine (with an enlarging glass), some of the pencil renderings included in the preceding pages and elsewhere to find other areas for experimentation.

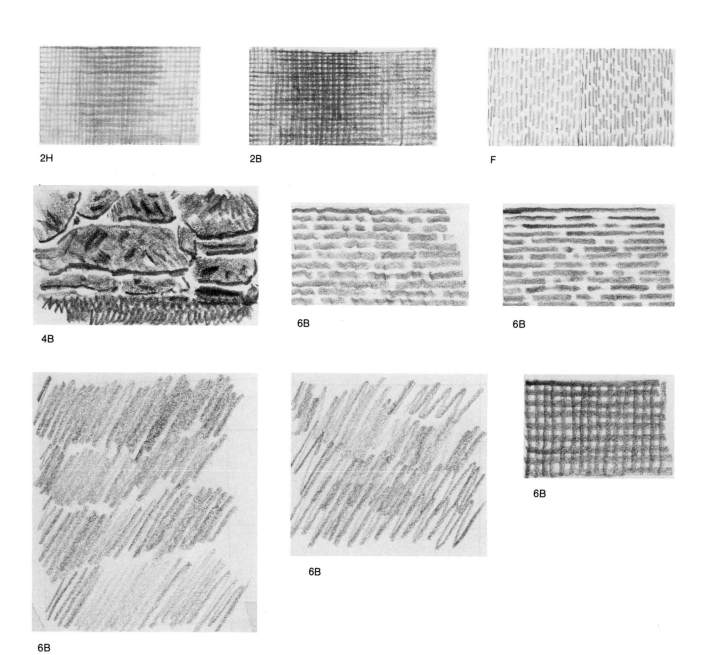

2H

2B

F

4B

6B

6B

6B

6B

6B

Typical strokes for pencil work.

Typical strokes for pencil work.

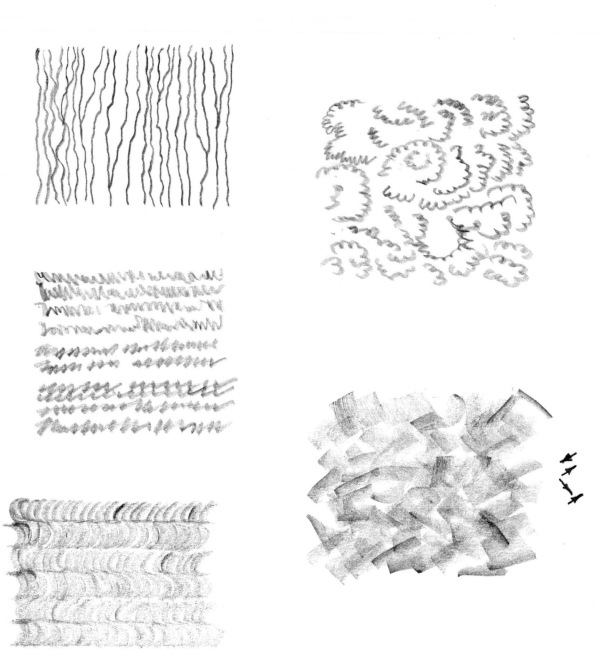

Typical strokes for pencil work.

Typical strokes for pencil work.

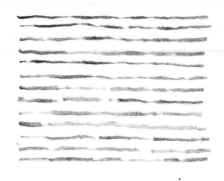

## TAILORS' CRAYONS

Developed originally for use by tailors to mark cloth bolts, tailors' crayons are useful to the renderer for laying in very large tonal areas. A graphite version, #900, is made by Dixon. Dixon #904 is the carbon version. Each is a slab approximately 2" square by 1/8" thick, tapering toward the bottom. The top half is covered with an enamel-like coating so the crayon can be manipulated without getting graphite or carbon all over the user's fingers. Producing a solid stroke 2" wide, it is particularly useful for laying in large areas of tone. The tailor's crayon is available also in three colors in a wax version. Graphite sticks about 1/4" × 1/2" × 3" are available in softer grades and these also can be used for filling in large areas of tone and can be notched to produce continuous lines and spaces.

The size of a rendering and the type of paper will determine the type and grade of pencil to use. Many renderers prefer refill pencils or various types of mechanical pencils over wood and graphite pencils because much time can be saved, and the annoyance of constant wood whittling avoided, by their use. A set of three or four filled with the most often-used grades of lead is handy. The hexagonal sides of the holder are marked with grades from 6H to 6B. Another solution to constant resharpening is the plastic-covered graphite stick, about 5/16" in diameter. Since high-quality pencils are expensive, it is also wise to have some pencil lengtheners on hand to make too-short stubs usable.

## CHARCOAL PENCILS

Because of its blackness, the charcoal pencil is much more useful than either graphite or carbon for covering large areas. Like the graphite pencil it can be smoothed with finger or paper stump. It is also available in four degrees ranging from hard to extra soft and in traditional stick form, also in various degrees of hardness. White chalk sticks are often used in conjunction with charcoal where sharp contrasts are desired.

Various ways to use charcoal. *Top left:* one application; next to that, finger application. *Bottom left:* two applications; and *right:* five applications with fixative between applications.

Typical strokes executed with a tailor's crayon.

## LITHOGRAPHIC PENCILS

The best-known lithographic pencil is that manufactured by William Korn. It is of soft greasy consistency which produces a rich black stroke on almost any surface—china, glass, stone, metal, and plastic, as well as on all kinds of paper. This paper-wrapped pencil comes in grades from 0 (softest) to 5 (hardest). Lithographic pencil lead may also be bought in stick form for use in mechanical pencils.

The lithographic pencil mark cannot be erased but can be scraped off with a razor blade. While these pencils require no fixative, the softer grades, in particular, are likely to rub off onto anything placed over them, so a little fixative will do no harm. Unless fixed, a lithographic pencil mark can be washed off of most hard surfaces. The lithographic pencil gets its name from the purpose for which it was first developed—drawing on the lithographic stone.

Cheaper versions of these pencils are known as grease pencils. While they have many of the advantages of the lithographic pencil, they are too greasy to make good drawing implements. However, adept renderers and architects have found their very disadvantages useful for some purposes. (See Paul Thiry's rendering in grease pencil on page 23).

## PASTEL PENCILS

Several manufacturers, including Koh-I-Noor, General, and Swan, produce pastel sticks in the form of pencils. These pencils are somewhat akin to charcoal pencils except that they are in color. Swan produces pastel pencils, under the trade name Carb-Othello, in sixty colors. Exactly matching pastel chalks in sixty colors are available to use with these.

WM KORN'S
LITHO
CRAYON

CONTÉ
CARRÉ'S
NOIRS

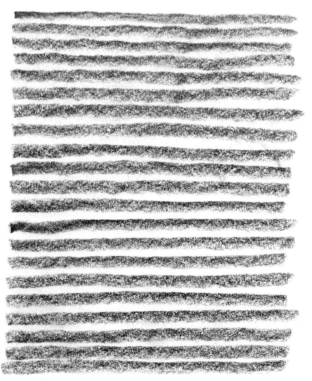

H. B. Wollf's carbon pencil.

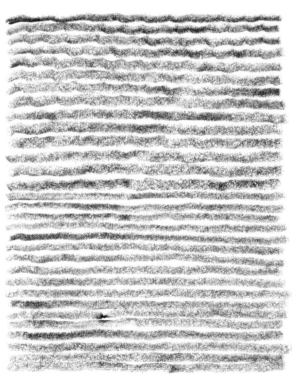

Negro pencil: #1 is used for the top half of the drawing, #3 for the bottom half.

# 3. THE PEN

Today the pen seems to be the favorite of a preponderance of architects for formal rendering and even for sketches. Several renderings in this book will prove, furthermore, that shades and shadows can be produced by pen as well as by pencil. Architects use every kind of pen for drawing, and while most prefer the more positive modern pens ranging from ball-points and India ink fountain pens through felt-tip pens and magic markers (even laundry markers), there will always be those who prefer the ink bottle and various crowquills, brushes, and a holder with various nibs for the very reason that they are not so positive—so perfect. Technical fountain pens are made by Koh-I-Noor and Staedtler but are almost universally referred to as Radiographs, a trade name of Koh-I-Noor. Actually, this firm makes another technical pen named the Acetograph with acid-resistant compound materials that permit the use of acetate inks as well as regular drawing and writing inks. Staedtler's pen is called the Mars. One model features an ink cartridge which is handy in the field. The other, like the Rapidograph, is a fountain pen.

California College of Podiatric Medicine, San Francisco. J. Merrell, renderer. The Rex Allen Partnership, Architects.

Ink and tempera rendering on heavy board. J. McBurney, renderer. Ralph Rapson and Associates, architects.

New York Telephone Co. Gino Misciagna, renderer. Griswold, Hecket & Kelly, Interior Designers.

STAR Center, Norwalk, Connecticut. Richard Bergmann, renderer and architect.

The use of pen and ink probaby does not reach as far back into antiquity as marking with chalk, slate, or other soft minerals. Nevertheless, the reed was used as a writing implement by Greek and Near Eastern writers from Roman times and, in fact, was known in Egypt and China around 2500 B.C. Later on the quill pen was developd and was common until quite recently—in this country right through the Civil War. Metal pens were not really of much consequence until the nineteenth century, but they were developed much earlier: a bronze pen much like those used before the fountain pen and ballpoint pen replaced them was found in the Tiber in ancient Rome. The first known steel pen was made in England in 1780 by Samuel Harrison in Birmingham. Machine-made pens appeared in 1822.

For the benefit of traditionalists and those who wish to experiment with real pens and real ink, an array of pens is available. At one time all master drawings had to be drawn on tracing cloth in ink. Straight and curved lines were drawn with a ruling pen while circles were executed with a compass fitted with a bow pen. Ruling pens have to be refilled frequently, so a bottle of drawing ink with a dispenser was a necessary adjunct. Some ink bottles have niblike protrusions from their corks from which ink can be dripped into the bow; others have eye-dropper arrangements so that ink can be drawn up from the bottle and discharged into the bow. These are all adjustable pens with a turn-screw for various line thicknesses and of course, they are still in wide use among draftsmen.

| Pentel sign pen | Rapidograph | Magic Marker | Flair | Brush |

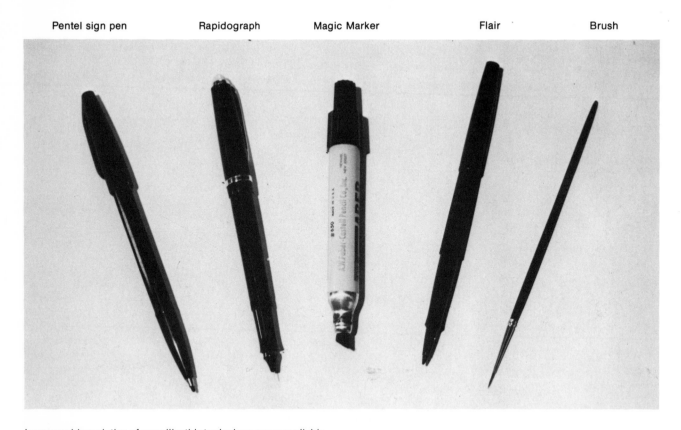

Innumerable varieties of pens like this typical group are available.

## POINT SIZES

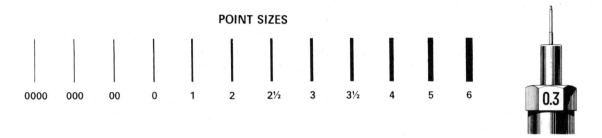

0000    000    00    0    1    2    2½    3    3½    4    5    6

0.3

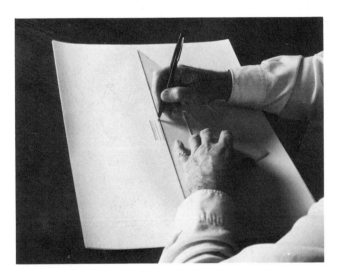

The technical fountain pen in the photograph is available with various point sizes, as shown above the photo.

The small brush (above) is handy for free forms while the Magic Marker (below) is for the bold stroke.

## HOW TO RENDER IN PEN AND INK

It is somewhat more difficult to achieve realistic tonal values in ink than in pencil. For that reason many renderers use the pen to outline the building and surroundings and fill in tones with the pencil. For the student it is just as important to try pen and ink as pencil, and, again, he should experiment with various pens and papers. A study with an enlarging glass of the renderings in the next section will add to the vocabulary of practice strokes. Younger folk never had the pleasure of working with the Palmer method of penmanship which was taught in schools a generation or two ago. It consisted of practicing a series of lines and loops until one could fill a page with these forms all exactly the same width, height, and consistency of spacing. It was a complete bore and was responsible for some of the most uni-formly dull handwriting ever known. It may have been responsible, in part, for the great lack of social correspondence from which we suffer today. The maddening thing is that the back of these penmanship books were quite another story. The same connected slanted lines and loops were combined to construct a variety of animals and other projects fascinating to the student. These, of course, were always ignored by the "penmanship" teacher.

Drill book practice can be dull, but there is no reason for the rendering student to fill whole pages with one or more pen-and-ink exercises. It would be better for the student to let his or her imagination rove a bit and try to combine his own forms with those shown here or those employed by the renderers.

Various straight line strokes are used here to establish the shade and shadow pattern that separates the interior from the exterior.

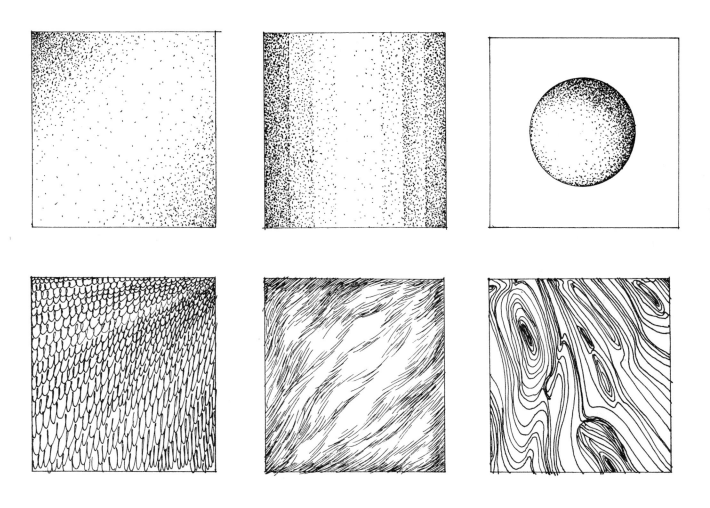

The drawings on top demonstrate that dots can be used for shading, as at left; for lines, as in the center; or to delineate, as at the right. At the bottom, note that lines can be used in many patterns—some repetitive, some not—to denote texture and shading.

Another method for toning ink drawings is to use graphic arts aids. An amazing variety of shading mediums, screens, and textures is available along with alphabets, numerals, arrows, symbols, rules, borders, and other special products. The best-known trade names are Bourges and Zippatone, but other trade names are Normatype, Letraset, Formatt, Deca-Dry, Spacematic, Prestype, and others. Some manufacturers offer pressure-sensitive tape which sometimes is used for lines on large drawings from which a 35 mm. slide is to be made. A wide variety of pressure-sensitive acetate film in color is available in matte and glossy finish. Transfer letters are well-known to architects; in fact, they are often used to excess. It is often assumed that a junior draftsman's time spent lettering a plan or other drawing is a lot cheaper than hand lettering or machine lettering, and this may be so. However, if there is any sizable amount of lettering, it is often even cheaper to have type set. Proofs can be pulled on tracing paper and taped to the drawing with magic transparent tape which will not show on a diazo print. Most pressure-sensitive acetate films, when properly applied, can be run through a diazo machine.

This progression shows the application of a piece of pressure-sensitive acetate over a drawing for shading. A piece slightly larger than the area to be covered is removed from the backing sheet and mounted over the object. Flatten it over—the art with the hand, then remove the excess with a matte knife. After this, cover the film with paper and burnish hard to firm adhesion.

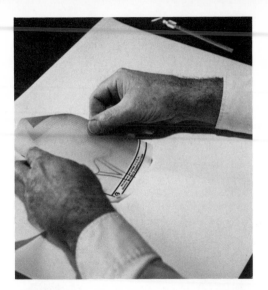

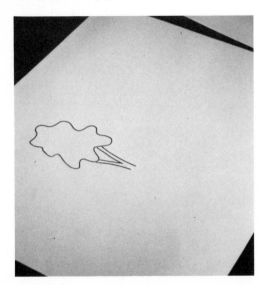

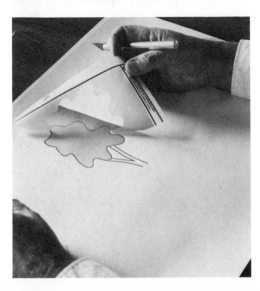

Many renderers have discovered that layers of paper can be used successfully for tonal effects. An example by a student is shown from a large file in the office of Herbert Gute of Yale. It is purely experimental, but it proves interesting results can come through the use of cheap and simple materials. The student first drew the outline of a simple building in sepia, placing it near the center of a 25″ × 29″ sheet of oriola. He added a couple of urns and a suggestion of bushes and trees, then cut the building shape out of a piece of blue-lined notebook paper to which a piece of cheesecloth had been glued. He mounted these inside his "building" form. He then added some bits of cheesecloth at the bottom, added a butterfly and some flowers cut from a magazine, and finally touched up with the sepia pen. The odd-looking agglomeration that is the original was then run through a diazo machine and the sepia print shown here was the result. The possibilities for effective use of double layers, applied material, and the like are clearly demonstrated by such an example.

BULAZEL

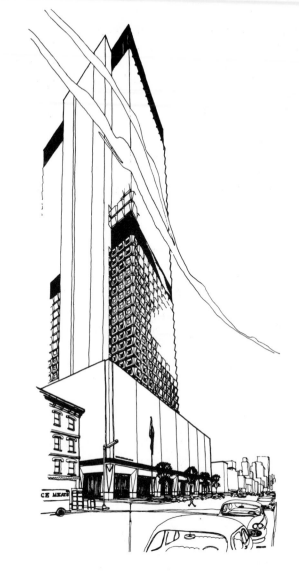

**Renderer:** Brian Burr
**Architects:** Castro-Blanco, Piscioneri, and Feder;
Gruzen & Partners Associated Architects
**Frawley Plaza** for New York State Urban
Development Corporation, Milbank Frawley Circle
110th Street and Fifth Avenue, New York

This is a presentation rendering approximately
20″ × 30″. The buildings, trees, and other entourage
were all executed in ink first. A sheet frisket was then
applied over the building forms and liquid mask
over areas where intricate tree forms meet the sky
or are reflected in the water in the foreground. Sky,
water, and background buildings were then air-
brushed. Most of the work around the windows of
the buildings was done with a pen. The only place
the pencil was employed was for tonal work, as a
close study of the drawing will show.

The New York State Urban Development Corporation requires a rendering of any project it under-
takes as a part of the design contract. Since a
photographic presentation like this is easy for the
layman to comprehend, Mr. Burr chose this
technique.

**Renderer:** Richard Bergmann
**Architect:** Max Urbahn Associates
**Franklin D. Roosevelt Branch,** U.S. Post Office,
Third Avenue, New York, N.Y.

The rendering was executed with Rapidograph
pen on vellum tracing paper, 20″ × 30″. Some people
familiar with New York may be slightly critical of the
number of trees visible only a block from Clarke's
Bar on Third Avenue, but that can be inked up to
artistic license. Actually, the variety of the New York
street scene is shown quite accurately.

**Renderer:** James Green Campbell
**Architects:** Desmond-Miremont-Burks
**CEBA Faculty Offices, Library, and Laboratories**

This rendering, executed on vellum, 24″ × 36″, was
drawn with a Rapidograph pen. It is a good example
of the possibilities for shading in using a fine-point
pen.

**Renderer:** Gerald Lee
**Architects:** Esherick, Homsey, Dodge and Davis
**Praia Grande** Portugal

A single rendering is often used as a basis for a whole slide presentation, as in this case. This makes it possible to show visually various aspects of the building, or complex, or simply the approach. The full rendering is shown and nine details are picked out and also shown. The full rendering was done with a Rapidograph on white tracing paper.

**Renderer:** D. C. Byrd
**Architect:** Marcel Breuer
**Breuer Cottage** 1948, Wellfleet, Massachusetts

How many of us get our first glimpse of a building we are anxious to see from the driver's seat of an automobile? Dale Byrd's pen and ink rendering presents this effective approach.

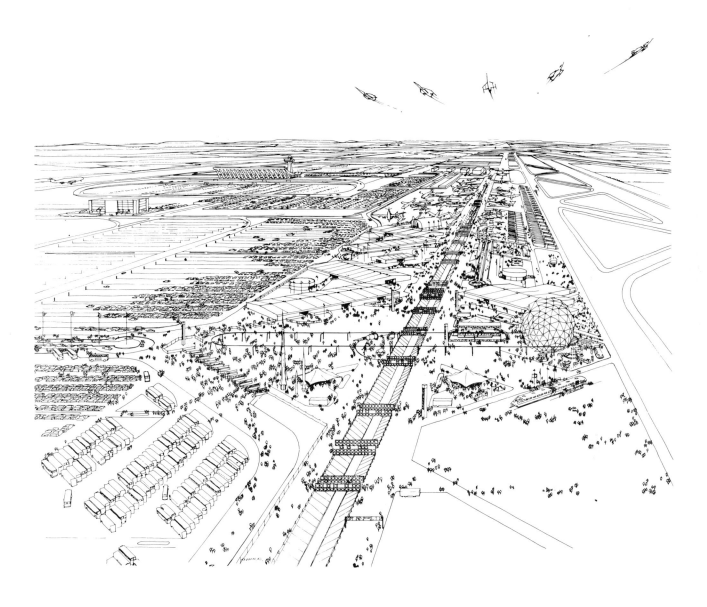

**Renderer:** Robert Kaminski
**Architects:** Welton Becket and Associates
**Transpo 72** Dulles International Airport
Washington, D.C.

Like Mr. Kaminski's pencil renderings on page 27, this rendering manages to convey great activity in the simplest kind of line treatment. It was rendered with a Rapidograph pen on a 30″ × 40″ illustration board.

**Renderer:** John G. Merrell
**Architects:** The Rex Allen Partnership
**Stanislaus Memorial** Modesto, California

This bird's-eye view in pen and ink has a full
range of tonal values.

**Renderer:** John Desmond
**Architect:** Desmond-Miremont-Burks

John Desmond is a virtuoso renderer with the pen. Here he has drawn, with a Rapidograph, a bird's-eye view using a variety of strokes to indicate tonal values. The original drawing was on smooth Strathmore, 30″ × 42″.

**Renderer:** Patrick Lopez
**Architect:** Skidmore, Owings & Merrill
**Sears Tower** Chicago, Illinois

Each of these drawings was executed in ink and airbrush on smooth illustration board, 17¼" × 29½". The figures in all three renderings are to the same scale so it is easy to see how the building will look to people approaching it from across the street, how it will look from the balcony surrounding the first-floor lobby, and what its effect will be on the skyline. It is possible with renderings to show as many parts of the building as one wishes in a way that is quite understandable to the merest layman. Mr. Lopez likes to see the commitment of an honestly drawn ink stroke. Other renderings by Mr. Lopez appear on page 11.

NORTHSIDE CENTER

**Renderer:** Gencheck
**Architects:** Castro-Blanco, Piscioneri and Feder; Gruzen and Partners, Associated Architects
**Frawley Plaza** for New York State Urban Development Corporation, Milbank Frawley Circle, 110th Street and Fifth Avenue, New York, N.Y.

This fine-line ink drawing is a freer rendition than the following view of the Madison Avenue Mall. It is from a station point slightly above the plaza and the figures in various locations give a good notion of its area.

**Renderer:** Bruce Johnson
**Planners:** van Ginkel Associates, Ltd.
**Madison Avenue Mall** New York, N.Y.

This view of Madison Avenue looking south toward the rectory of St. Patrick's Cathedral between East 50th and 51st Streets was executed in black ink on white board, 12½″ × 24″. The perspective was "eyeballed" from photographs of the site.

Statement from van Ginkel Associates:

This office does not use any computer perspectives. What seems important with a perspective is not so much mechanical accuracy but the visual perceptual accuracy, such as the use of light and conveyance of ambience.

The renderings on these pages are in two very distinctive styles; the impressionistic one by Mr. Gencheck requires the most imagination on the part of the viewer while Mr. Johnson's rendering depends for its realism on the detail in the buildings in the foreground on either side of 51st Street.

**Renderer:** F. Nemeth
**Architect:** Sverdrup & Parcel and Associates, Inc.,
Engineers-Architects
Rapson A.I.A. Architects, Consulting Architect
**Federal Office Building** General Services Administration, St. Louis, Missouri

The original of this drawing was on tracing paper, 30″ × 40″. Mr. Nemeth's rendering is actually a very realistic picture. He employed a felt pen for the perspective of his buildings and used the pencil for its tonal qualities.

**Renderer:** Gordon Brown
**Architects:** Brown & Brown
**Residence**

This sketch was rendered with a marking pen on white illustration board, 9″ × 16″, for in-house study and discussion with the client.

Arthur Brown, founder of the firm and of the renderer, has this to say about presentation methods:

Of all the methods of presentation, I prefer the felt pen since it is the fastest and seems to reproduce best. This may be used in conjunction with watercolor, plain pastel, or if used on a suede surface, oil pastel works best.

I prefer water-soluble ink since it blends with the watercolor and simplifies the lines. Where lines are wanted, the watercolor should touch only one side of the line. The water-soluble ink is best used on the suede board also since the waterproof ink has a solvent which is likely to pick up the nap on suede.

Most architects are too busy to make a mechanical perspective. It is easier to draw a few construction lines and do it by guess. This can be done in a fourth of the time it takes to make a mechanical layout.

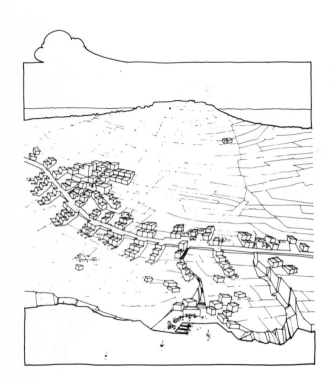

**Renderer:** Charles B. Zucker
**Architects:** Baker and Blake
**Italian Riviera Resort**

This intriguing series was executed on single-sided Mylar, 14″ square. The renderer worked with #0, #2, and #4 Rapidograph pens on a constructed perspective using the Jay Doblin technique. The renderings were reduced to 8″ square and used in a publicity brochure for the project.

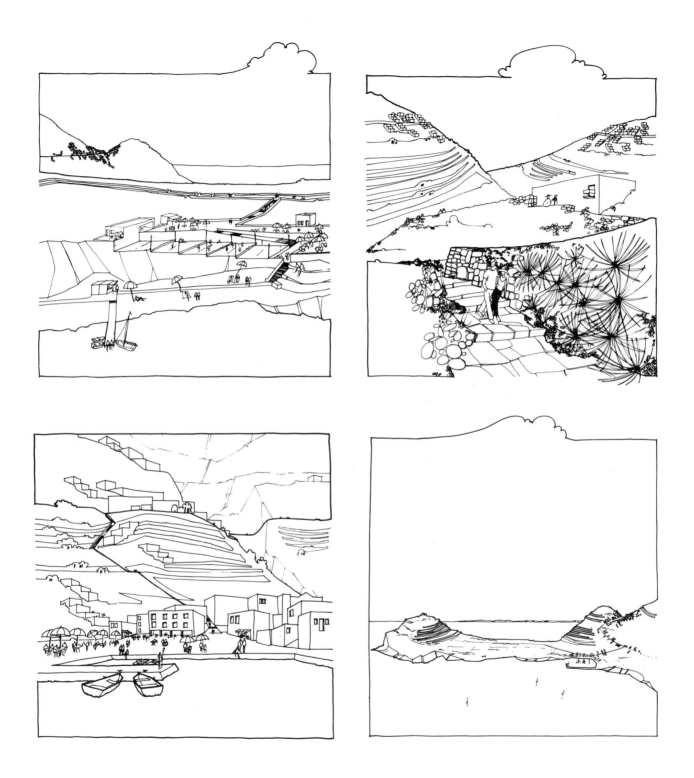

**Renderer:** Gino Misciagna
**Interior Designers:** Griswold, Heckel and Kelly
**New York Telephone Company Offices** New York,
N.Y.

Gino Misciagna's ink-line base drawing of the
New York Telephone Company's conference room
is shown here and a color version of the same
drawing is in the color section. To see what the
addition of a few simple colors will do to this drawing, turn to the color version in the color section.

**Renderer:** Shung M. Louie
**Architects:** Welton Becket and Associates
**Clinton Square Development** Syracuse, New York

The original of this ink drawing was on double weight #80 Bainbridge board, 24″ × 35″. It was rendered especially to be reproduced frequently in various sizes for distribution to the people of the city. It was done by tracing over a photograph of a study model and placing the new buildings into their site with information gathered from photographs of the site. A unique and simple brochure designed to display Mr. Louie's talents both as a delineator and an architect is shown on page 162.

**Renderer:** Harry Weese
**Architect:** Harry Weese & Associates
**The Latin School of Chicago** Chicago, Illinois

Essentially a pencil rendering on yellow tracing
paper, this example, is included here because the
shading was added with a felt pen.

**Renderer:** Harry Weese
**Architect:** Harry Weese & Associates
**Caribbean Pavilion** Interama, Miami, Florida

This rendering was executed with a Gillott 303 pen and shaded with Drawing Technical. It is on 20″ × 30″ illustration board. The broken reflection of the building in the foreground water is particularly intriguing.

**Renderer:** Harry Weese
**Architect:** Harry Weese & Associates
**North Clark–LaSalle Street Redevelopment Project** Chicago, Illinois

This very free rendering in ink on 20″ × 30″ illustration board, when reduced as above, is a very effective picture of an intimate residential development in which each unit has its own garden and a small common is shared.

**Renderers:** Tan & Voss
**Architect:** Frank LLoyd Wright
**Architects for the renovation and restoration:**
Skidmore, Owings & Merrill
**Robie House** Chicago, Illinois

Aside from Falling Water, the Kaufman house outside Pittsburgh, the Robie house is probably one of Wright's most notable houses. This rendering of the interior is executed on board, approximately 24″ × 36″, in pen and mixed media. A rendering of the exterior by Joseph F. Hennessy appears on page 35.

**Renderer:** Joseph F. Hennessey
**Architect:** Robert F. Mall & Associates
**Proposed Summit School** Dundee, Illinois

The flat magic marker would seem to be an extremely difficult tool to master and this rendering shows fantastic control over it. Almost every stroke in this rendering was made with this instrument, with long strokes used in the sky and short choppy strokes for the foliage. The building itself is nearly all controlled magic marker stroke. Some of the small detailing, like the people and details near the building must have been put in with a felt-tip pen. The original, on 1000 H tracing paper, was approximately 10½″ × 24″.

**Renderers:** Eric Mendelsohn & Gino Misciagna
**Architect:** Eric Mendelsohn
**Einstein Tower** Astro-Physical Institute, Potsdam,
Germany, 1920

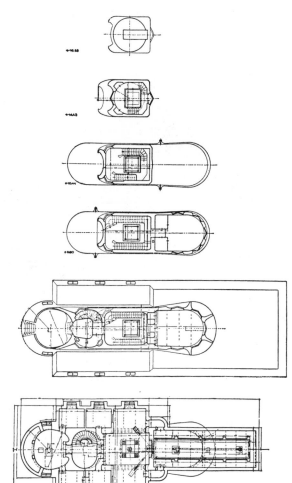

The late Eric Mendelsohn's ability to describe a
building with a few well-placed strokes was un-
canny. It was possible because after familiarizing
himself with the site, he made perspective sketches
from all points of view. Here is Mendelsohn's early
study of the Einstein Tower with the six-floor plans
under it. Accompanying it is Gino Misciagna's re-
cent rendering of it. Here was Misciagna's procedure:

1. The base drawing was done on #80 Bainbridge illustration board #2, 30″ × 40″, with tooth.
Using brown ink in a 00 Rapidograph pen, the
renderer completed the drawing as though he were
executing a watercolor. The tones in the sky, foreground, and tree at the right were accomplished by
applying liquid mask with a ruling pen or a brush,
depending on the area. The masked area included
the building and foreground grass as well as the
entourage on either side of the building.

2. The board was saturated with water, and large
toned areas were painted with a sepia wash. The
next step, removing the masks, could not be taken
until the board had dried completely. This would
take at least a day, possibly longer, depending on
the climate. If the paper is not completely dry, the
surface of the paper will pull off when the liquid
mask is removed.

3. The same masking material was applied over
the previously painted area and the same process
was followed down to the details of the leaves and
rocks which provide highlights in the drawing.

# 4. PERSPECTIVE

The principles of perspective were understood in the early part of the fifteenth century. Filippo Brunelleschi (1377–1446), a Florentine architect and engineer, may have been the earliest experimenter, but it is to Piero della Francesca (1420–1492), an Umbrian painter, that the attribution of the conception of the vanishing point, the key to perspective construction, has been given. Leonardo da Vinci (1452–1519), Baldassarre Peruzzi (1481–1536), and Michelangelo Buonarroti (1475–1564), all Florentines, certainly understood perspective. Reproduced here is a sheet from a Michelangelo sketchbook with a building elevation, rather carelessly framed by some anatomical sketches. The fanciful Peruzzi sketch is perspectively correct.

Orthographic projection (also known as descriptive geometry), which is infinitely simpler to work with than mechanical perspective, did not come along until nearly the end of the eighteenth century when it was discovered by a French mathematician and physicist, Gaspard Monge (1746–1818). This progression is strange because perspective is much more complex and permits the viewer to see the object in three dimensions while in orthographic drawing only two dimensions can be seen in any one view.

Michelangelo Buonarroti, 1475—1564.

Baldassarre Peruzzi, 1481—1537.

Oblique drawing is very useful to the architect because it enables him to see through a space, which helps indicate the positional relationships of different planes. The planes shown retain their true shape while all other planes are distored to indicate the depth of the object.

An isometric drawing is the easiest to draw because in it all planes are distorted equally and at the same angle. Therefore, also, the depth of the object is measured accurately.

The mystery of the Sphinx is matched only by the mystery of why ancient Egyptian drawings and even bas-reliefs are always flat. One explanation is that when the pyramids were being built by slave labor, the enormous blocks were lifted manually by the slaves with some help coming from makeshift block and tackle arrangements. When the weight got to be too much for the slaves, or when the poor quality of the rope caused it to fall, these enormous blocks often fell on slaves and pharoahs alike. Thus, according to this theory, the Egyptians actually *were* flat.

Countering this explanation is the more mundane academic one that the Egyptians did not understand perspective. Indeed, there are probably many more people today who do not understand perspective than there ever were before in its history. In a book published in 1930 and carrying the title *Perspective Projection*, the author, Ernest Irving Freese, on his dedication page portrays himself at the drawing board in the evocative sketch typical of the period. Under it is the comment: ". . . it has taken more than two thousand years to produce this little book . . ." The book's subtitle is *A Simple and Exact Method of Making Perspective Drawings.* Fortunately, over the past forty-odd years since the Freese book, many methods have been devised that are exact enough and considerably simpler. There are many excellent books on traditional and newly devised methods of perspective projection, and those the author feels are most useful are included in the Bibliography.

The author is fortunate to have obtained some sketches on the perspective of trees from Herbert Gute, who teaches both art and architectural students at Yale. He has found that when the architects first come to his studio they do a superb job on the building, but when the time comes for some imaginative freehand work—trees, people, grass, cars, and other such things—they are lost. Of all the things God made, the tree must be the most difficult to draw. Mr. Gute explains in this series of drawings that the branches of trees are either Y-shaped or triangular. For a tree to be three-dimensional it must have branches coming toward the viewer from various points in the trunk and among the branches themselves. Furthermore, a tree should follow the laws of perspective, as he shows in these sketches. In the lower branches the horizontal dimension is dominant, while in the upper branches the vertical dominates. This rule continues to apply as the second and third row of branches are added. Mr. Gute says that he is not interested here in a tree as a tree but as a system, and the Y branches are rotated through space up and down—right and left. The lower series of sketches explains how the gradient phenomenon operates on trees. It has long been known that as depth increases, we see more. Looking at a town from a distance, for instance, we can count many more buildings than we can when we move closer to the town. The closer we get, the fewer buildings we see. The drawing at the bottom right diagrams how this principle works with trees. There appear to be more branches at the top and bottom than in the center. Similarly with leaf lines: There seem to be be more on the outside edges than in center. The umbrella sketch establishes the concept of light and shadow on trees. The middle sketch shows how the gradient principle applies to a tree. There are more and larger holes in the center vertically and horizontally as well as left to right. It is interesting to study the renderings in this book to see how rarely otherwise realistic-looking trees include a third dimension.

The only short course in perspective in this volume will be found in the discussion on computer perspective in the last chapter. Occasionally, a renderer whose work is included in this book will divulge his favorite method. More and more often, a lot of drudgery is avoided by establishing picture plane, station point, and vanishing points through the use of a photograph at the site, a simple (or complicated) model, or a combination of the two.

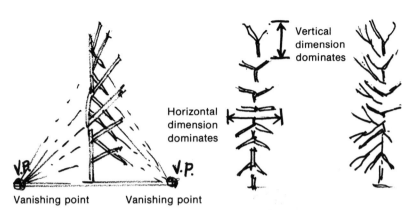

Vertical dimension dominates

Horizontal dimension dominates

Vanishing point     Vanishing point

| | | | | |
|---|---|---|---|---|
| Perspective | One row of branches | Two rows | Three | Triangle-shaped branch |

Tree: membrane and gradient

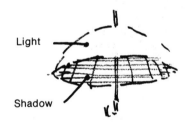

Light

Shadow

Concept

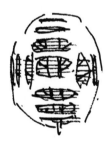

Front and back membrane
2 Holes gradient

Leaf lines
Gradient

Gradient

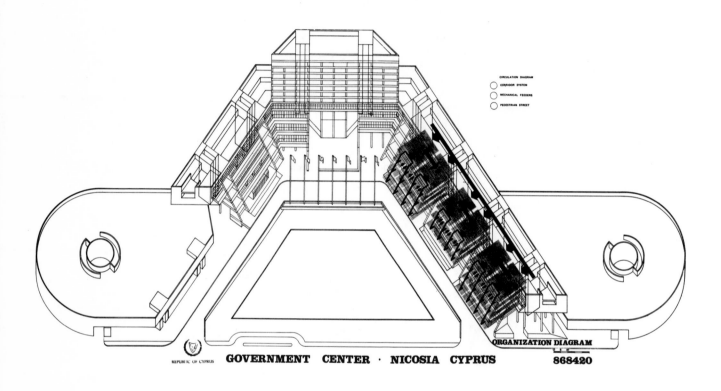

CIRCULATION DIAGRAM
○ CORRIDOR SYSTEM
○ MECHANICAL FEEDERS
○ PEDESTRIAN STREET

ORGANIZATION DIAGRAM

REPUBLIC OF CYPRUS · **GOVERNMENT CENTER · NICOSIA CYPRUS** 868420

**Renderer:** John Sheehy, Valdis Smits
**Architects:** The Architects Collaborative
**Government Center** Nicosia, Cyprus

This oblique drawing is a part of a complete presentation of 32 sheets. All are 18⅝″ × 27¼″ including the black and white portion of this sheet, except
five which were 18⅝″ × 40¼″, with each side folding
in 6½″. The first basic drawing shows all levels
while the toned sections and arrows are actually a
clear film overlay which, when added to the basic
drawing, shows the functional relationships.

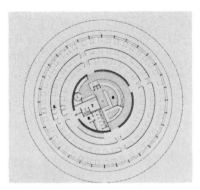

Dining room level plan

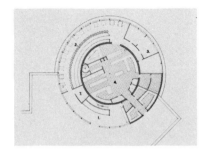

Entrance level plan

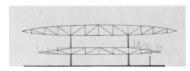

Section

PLAN KEY
1. LOBBY - AQUARIUM
2. RAW BAR
3. PRIVATE DINNING ROOM
4. KITCHEN
5. DINNING ROOM
6. SERVING PANTRY
7. MEN'S RESTROOM
8. WOMEN'S RESTROOM

West elevation

**Renderer:** E. H. Niles, Jr.
**Architects:** The Architectural Affiliation; Christie, Niles and Andrews
A Plan for the **Inner Harbor** Baltimore, Maryland

These drawings are part of a thesis presentation by E. H. Niles of a scheme devised to take heavy shipping out of Baltimore's inner harbor, rehabilitate a slum business area, and create three versions of water and its possible uses: A canal water garden leading from the harbor directly to the plaza in front of City Hall, a vertical jet and fountains, and lastly the harbor itself. As part of the latter, the architects planned a basin for small boating and ancillary facilities. The part of the presentation shown here is the restaurant, round in shape to recall the lantern of a lighthouse. Drawings include entrance and restaurant level plans, a section, a rendering of the restaurant itself and of the restaurant in relation to part of the marina, and, for historical reference, the ship *Constellation*, the pride of Baltimore in an earlier day. Part of the ship is visible at the right in the rendering.

As renderer, Mr. Niles executed these drawings on illustration board, 20" × 30". The basic medium was tempera used in a ruling pen for most of the straight-line work, and in a dilute wash for coloration of water, sky, foliage, and the like. A crowquill pen and a small Speedball were used for pilings, figures, and other freehand details.

The restaurant

**Renderer:** Alexi Vergun
**Architects:** Marcel Breuer and Herbert Beckhard
**House on Lake Maggio** Tessin, Switzerland

The elevation the renderer presents here faces
the lake. This drawing illustrates how effectively
a simple elevation can be employed to depict a
rather complex building.

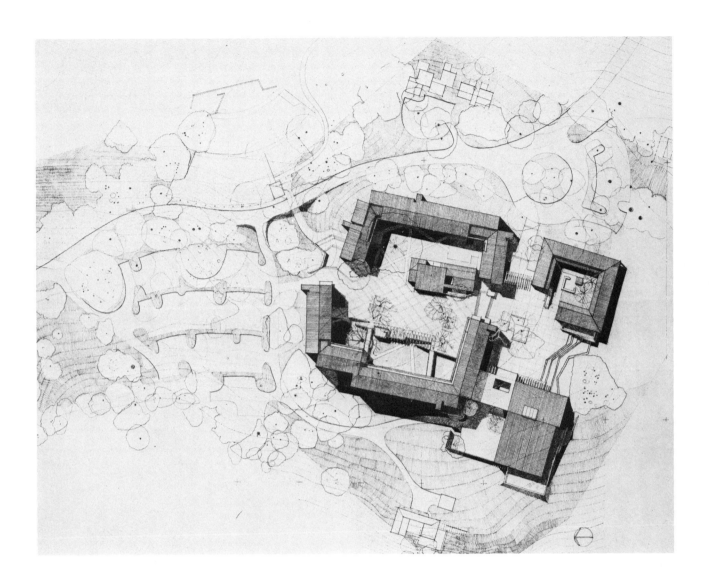

**Renderer:** Hugh Stubbins
**Architects:** Hugh Stubbins and Associates, Inc.
**Roof Plan** College No. 5, University of California, Santa Cruz, California

This drawing was rendered on a sepia print, approximately 16″ × 20″, with Prismacolor pencils. When used in conjunction with other drawings or a model, it helps orient people who are trying to understand a large project.

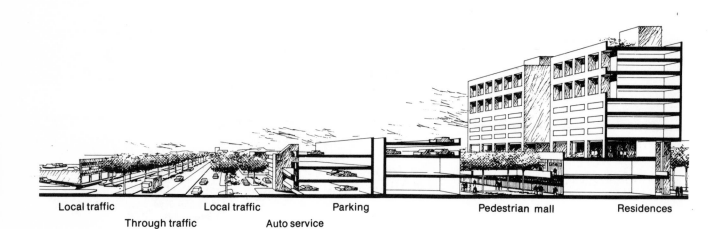

Local traffic      Local traffic      Parking      Pedestrian mall      Residences

Through traffic      Auto service

**Renderer:** Mark Ueland
**Architects:** Ueland and Junker

Design for a Suburban Arterial Road and an Adjacent Center for Shopping, Offices, and Residences, Montgomery County Community Renewal Program, Montgomery County, Maryland

Here the renderer's perspective section presents an effective solution to a very complex set of requirements. Two other renderings by Mr. Ueland appear on pages 150 and 151.

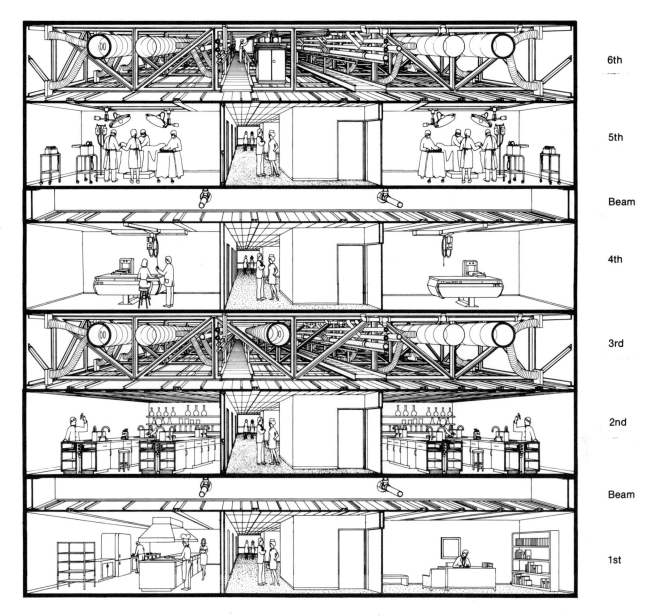

6th

5th

Beam

4th

3rd

2nd

Beam

1st

**Renderer:** John G. Merrell
**Architects:** The Rex Allen Partnership
**Sacred Heart Hospital** (Systems Floors) Eugene, Oregon

The systems floors in a hospital (also called interstitial spaces) are those floors housing mechanical, electrical, and heating and air-conditioning systems. To create the section shown here, the original of the one-point perspective drawings are inked on 6″ × 36″ strips. The strips are then mounted on large sheets from which clear Mylar contact positives are made. Selected floors are cut from the Mylar prints which contain numerous variations of floor types; these are assembled and taped together. This art work serves as a master from which a variety of graphic reproductions can be made.

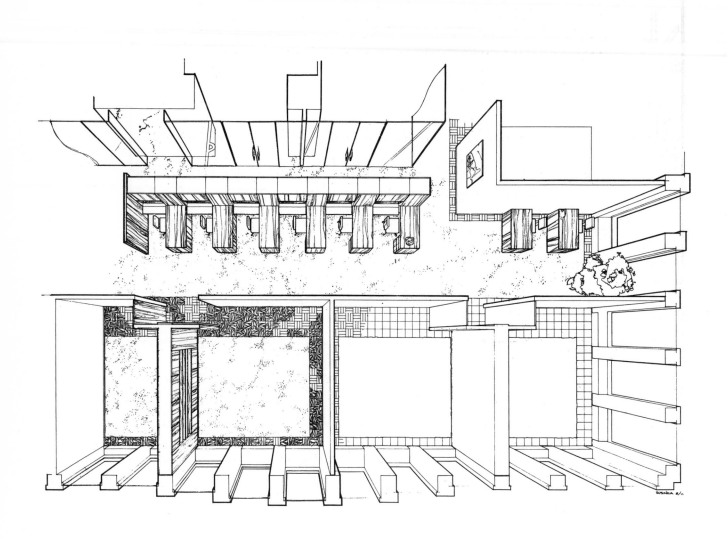

**Architects:** Skidmore, Owings & Merrill
**One Shell Plaza—Interior** Houston, Texas

A one-point bird's-eye perspective can be very effective in showing furniture arrangement and other details of an interior. This drawing was rendered in ink on a 30″ × 40″ board.

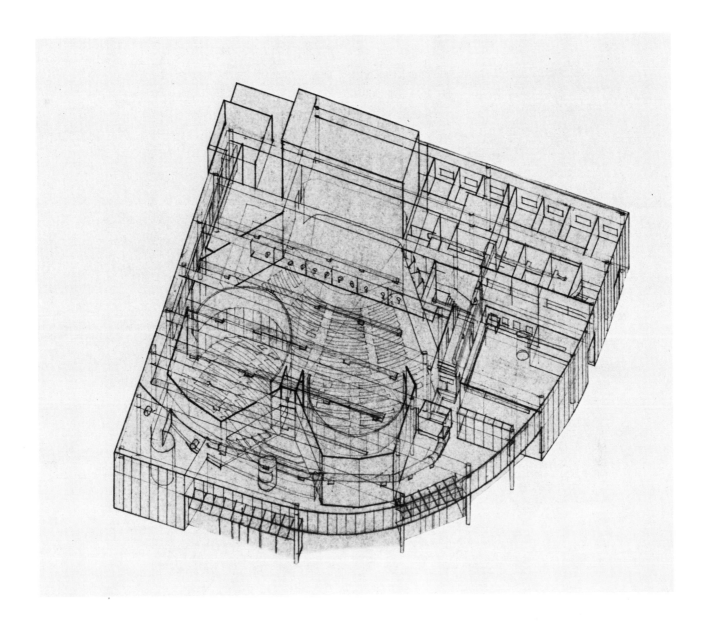

**Renderer:** Thomas Larson
**Architect:** The Architects Collaborative
**Westbrook Fine Arts Center** 1972, Portland, Maine

An oblique drawing like this pencil one is useful
for office study. Executed by setting the plan at the
best viewing angle and then generating it vertically,
it was used to study interior volumes in relation to
the exterior membrane.

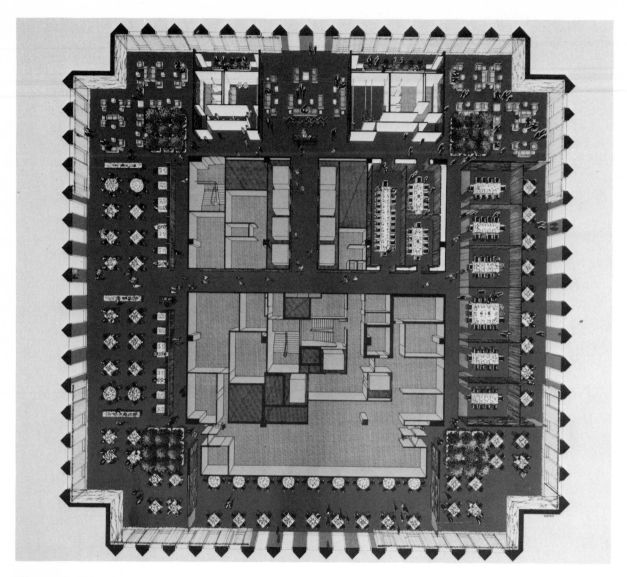

**Renderer:** Beatrice Aaron
**Architects:** Skidmore, Owings & Merrill
**Mid-America Club** Standard Oil Building, Chicago,
Illinois

While normally an oblique perspective might be
difficult for the layman to read, this dramatic presentation certainly would not be. The rendering
was silk-screened on bronze Plexiglas, 30″ square,
in white, rust, and light olive, but its dramatic quality is not lost even in a black and white reproduction.

96

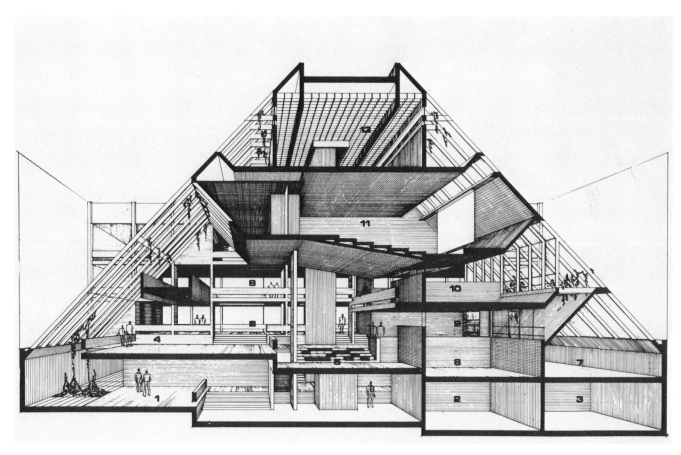

**Renderer:** Martin Holub
**Architect:** Martin Holub
**Competition Design for Architectural Association
Building** London, England

One-point perspective is ideal for this essentially simple building because it is possible, with it, to show the rather complex interrelations between the spaces. The drawing was executed on tracing paper, using ink for the line work and walls and ceiling. A pencil was used to differentiate between areas that were open and those with glass in filling. Another of Mr. Holub's drawings is reproduced on page 20.

Key:
1. Basement cloakroom & toilet lobby
2. Staff lockers   3. Kitchen stores   4. Exhibition space
5. Informal discussion "pit"   6. Restaurant   7. Kitchen
8. Library   9. General common bar
10. C.A.S.E. lecture room   11. Lecture theatre
12. Access to workshop/Laboratories
13. Studio-Theater

**Delineators:** Douglas Cooper (Job Captain); Damion Austin; Sir John Banks; Chuck Culbertson, Jay Greenfield; Sharon Kecton; Joe Nagy; Robert Phipps; Emily Eckel; Sanders Woodall; Troy West
**Architects:** Troy West, Community Design Associates
**Study for Department of Transportation** Hill District, Pittsburgh, Pennsylvania

An unusually dramatic method of presenting a study, this map is 24′ × 40′—large enough to walk on. It was made up in 18″ × 24″ panels on the stiff drawing paper of Grumbacher all-purpose Artcraft sketch pad. The medium used by the delineators was black, sky-blue, and green poster paint.

Before the map was made, Mr. West and Mr. Cooper walked the streets of the Hill District. They hired local residents as consultants to take photographs and otherwise help in the documentation. The architects felt, correctly as it turned out, that a map of this size would be sufficiently understood by the people in the area so that they could participate in the planning process. The laid-out map is shown and also two enlarged sections of it.

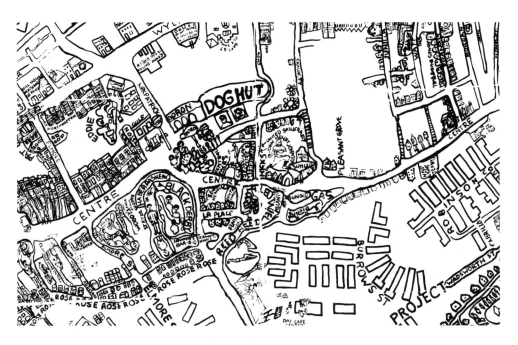

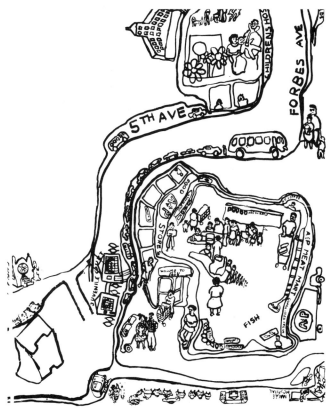

**Renderer:** Troy West
**Architects:** Troy West, Community Design
Associates
**Proposal for Housing** Pittsburgh, Pennsylvania

This very free section drawing was executed in
charcoal and pastel on clear print 1000 H vellum
tracing paper, 27″ × 36″. The legend at the right
reads: "Plant a tree and then build a house tall as
the tree and then let the tree come in the house."

**Renderer:** Joseph Esherick
**Architects:** Esherick, Homsey, Dodge and Davis
**Sea Ranch Houses**

Mr. Esherick's rough studies clearly transmit to his staff what he has in mind from the point of view of plan and sections. The originals of these sketches were executed with pens on brown construction paper, approximately 8″ × 10″.

# 5. COMPOSITION

The *American Heritage Dictionary* defines the word composition as "A putting together of parts or elements to form a whole; a combining." The ability to compose a picture, whether a photograph, a painting or a rendering is either intuitive or becomes so through long experience.

The center of interest in an architectural rendering is, with rare exceptions, a building, a complex of buildings, or building interiors. The same is true of photomontage presentations or of photographs of models. Therefore, unlike the artist, the renderer does not have a very hard decision to make regarding subject matter. He does have a problem, and it can be a real one, of how to make his new building stand out without being too obvious—especially if the building is in a cityscape. Those exceptions where no building is involved are more difficult to compose. The Madison Avenue Mall on page 71 and Transpo 72 on page 65 are examples of this kind of problem.

An important rule of composition is the principle of proportion—that is, the relation of the whole composition to the size of the paper it is drawn on or the relation of one part of a drawing to another. When a great deal of detail is to be shown, a large sheet is required—15″ × 20″ or larger. The larger the sheet, generally speaking, the heavier the pencil or pen strokes. Such large drawings are then reduced, without loss of detail, to slides or for reproduction in magazines and newspapers. Where the primary aim is impact, detail becomes unimportant and smaller drawings will serve just as well.

The first drawing illustrates the importance of keeping the principal element—in this case the building—dominant. It also illustrates what is usually a poor practice; placing the horizon line in the very center of the composition. Although, in this

case, the drawing succeeds because of the hills in the background, it is usually better to locate the horizon line slightly above or below dead center.

In this drawing the building at the left is the center of interest, while the buildings at the right and behind it are supporting elements employed to place the principal building in its setting. Here the horizon line is higher than average, but still at a fairly normal level for cityscapes.

The horizon line in this drawing is above the center and we are given a bird's-eye view of the building. It is important in considering viewpoint (or station point) in any drawing that it be a normal and natural one. Some examples of this principle are to be found in the Breuer house rendering by

D. C. Byrd (p. 64), the New York Telephone Company facility in Grand Central Terminal by Granville Ackermann (p. 24), and the three houses by Norman Jaffe (p. 30 and in the color section on page 179). In this drawing, when the approach is by land, it is most often from above the house, so this is a normal view. Architecturally speaking, it is interesting that in cases of this kind the roof is rarely considered as a design element. Viewed from beneath, as this house would be if approached by water, the design elements would be more interesting.

Here, as in the first house sketch, the horizon line is near the center of interest of the picture. This sketch also illustrates a valuable method for cityscapes whereby a new building can be emphasized while surroundings, even in the foreground, can be muted.

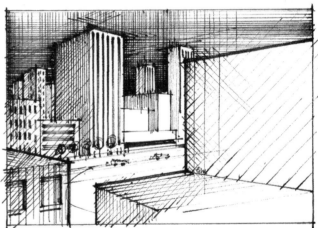

These sketches by Gino Misciagna (who also provided all the other ones in this chapter), are examples of placement of the center of interest ranging from middle ground (A), to background (B), and foreground (C). The center of interest in a bird's-eye view, with the building in the background, makes a statement to the effect that "I'm here to change this neighborhood." In a well-conceived drawing, everything else recedes to makes this possible. The middle-ground approach is often used in cityscapes to indicate how a new building harmonizes with the surrounding buildings in the area. It has something like an eaves-dropping effect, as though looking over other buildings to view this one, which is the center of interest in the composition. With the new building in the foreground, the client is likely to feel it dominates its surroundings, which is exactly what he usually wants it to do. Gino Misciagna calls it the "virtuoso syndrome," which can be used to convince the entrepreneur of the importance of his project.

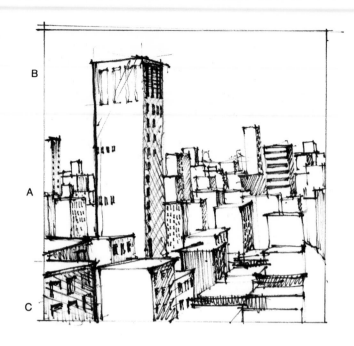

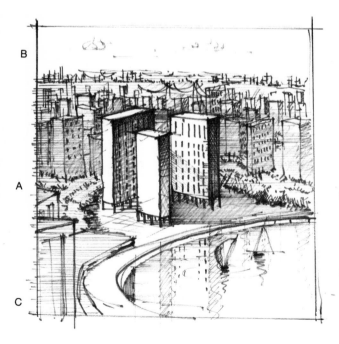

A long, low building such as depicted in these two drawings should obviously be rendered the long way of the paper. In the sketch where the house runs horizontally, the tree at right is used to help frame the composition. Another such element at the left would tend to disturb the rhythm of the drawing. The foliage above and to the left of the house provide ample framing here. The house also becomes a more important element in the composition when the picture plane is turned on its side and brought closer to it.

The principles of unity and balance are closely related. When all of the elements of a composition are properly balanced, equilibrium results and each element, including the center of interest, retain its own attractive force. If one or more of the elements are fighting for supremacy, the composition is not balanced and will also lack unity.

The building should not be lost in the entourage, as it tends to be in the sketch with the evergreen. However, entourage can be used successfully so the architect can present a concept rather than a detailed study of the finished work. In the second sketch the same building so dominates the composition that it cries out for supporting elements.

The third sketch is an example of a well-balanced composition which, at the same time, is a unified whole. The fact that the eye tends to move in a clockwise direction when viewing a picture is illustrated here. Because of this, the eye is brought to the center of interest even though the supporting elements—the tree, the dock, the rowboat, the sailboat, and the birds—are quite evident. This sketch also proves that blank spaces are an important element in achieving balance.

The principle of contrast is illustrated by the circle outlined by a decreasingly gray surround. This sketch also illustrates one way to achieve values in an ink drawing. John Desmond's rendering (p. 67) epitomizes the use of this kind of ink work for value. The renderings from the office of Venturi and Rauch on page 122 illustrate how contrast and value can be attained using vertical lines not only for rectilinear shapes but for curves as well.

No matter what medium is employed, the employment of solid black against stark white can be used to good advantage. This method is often used in site plans as a means of achieving solidity in a drawing with a minimum of drawing effort. In elevations, it accentuates irregularities of a facade surface. Contrasts of this kind are also important in achieving movement and clarity in a facade. Applying Zippatone to drawings of this kind will add tones where necessary. The sketch shown here might merely be a study in contrasts, but it is not difficult to imagine it as a series of circular buildings with straight and curved links connecting them.

The principle of contrast is as important to a composition as are unity and balance. A flat, gray photograph of a building taken on a dull day lacks contrast. While every feature of the building may be discernible, and all other elements recognizable, nothing stands out against anything else. Sharp color contrast can be used to define a form clearly and relate it to its environment. Contrast can be used powerfully for impact or subtly for informational purposes. Contrast also can be used to achieve perspective in a composition, with darks in the foreground and lights in the background (or vice versa). Light colors and tones tend to come forward, darks to recede. In a painting, contrast is used to achieve chiaroscuro. Watercolorists like Ted Kautzky and renderers like Ernest Born use contrast beautifully.

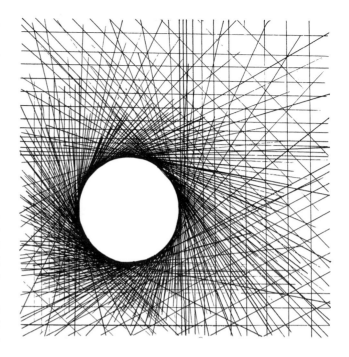

# 6. ARCHITECTS' DRAWINGS

The drawings on the next few pages are the products of architects who just enjoy drawing—a very evident fact. The drawing on page 109 by A. Quincy Jones is one of hundreds he has produced on trips to various parts of the world. He sends a sepia print of an enlarged verson (31″ × 40″) of one of his drawings each year as a holiday greeting card. It arrives in a mailing tube and is immediately hung on the wall. This one was drawn in Taxco, Mexico.

Tasco Mex. 14 May 1992

Theodore J. Musho is a senior associate in the firm of I. M. Pei & Partners, Architects. The first two drawings are the Campidoglio—Palazzo Senato and the interior of Santa Costanza. The next two are Campidoglio—Palazzo Conservatori and the interior of Santa Maria in Cosmedin. The originals are approximately 29″ × 40″ and were drawn when Mr. Musho was a Fellow of the American Academy in Rome.

Norman Jaffe's five finished drawings were made in Stockholm in acrylic on watercolor paper. Mr. Jaffe provides us with notes on his procedure:

1. I first make notes on a small-scale sketch (5¼" × 7"), as in the first drawing. These are made quickly, only recording the essence of the scene.
2. Then I leave before getting bogged down in details.
3. I look at my notes away from the place I sketched and try to compose in the abstract.
4. I lay in the background washes in my hotel room. They dry; this may take considerable time, depending on weather.
5. I return to the scene and react to the forms, rapidly laying in the lines with a felt-tip pen.

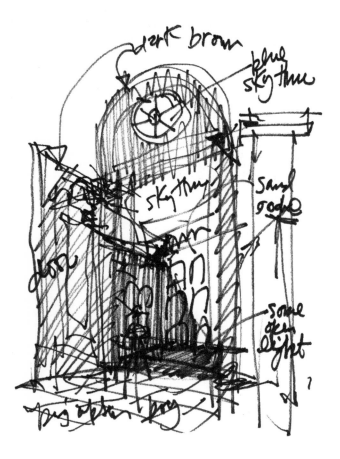

Thomas Larson, now an associate with The Architects Collaborative in Boston and also Visiting Critic in Architecture at Harvard, made these sketches in India and Japan while on a Rotch Traveling Scholarship and an A.I.A. scholarship. The originals are on 11″ × 17″ rag newsprint using brown and black ink mixed. With the Indian drawings, time was a major factor and he found the Flomaster the fastest method for capturing sun and shadow of mass volumes. Many of the compounds cannot be photographed.

In this cityscape by John Desmond of Desmond-
Miremont-Burks in New Orleans, it is interesting to
compare the freedom of execution with the careful
line technique displayed by Mr. Desmond in his ink
rendering on page 67.

# 7. PHOTOGRAPHY AND PHOTOPROJECTION

The camera and slide projector have become as much a part of making architectural presentations as pencils, pens, paper, ink, watercolor, and other media. The presentation by Ben Althen in this chapter of the Pacific Centre is a print of a photo negative on photo mural paper twice the size of the original. Several renderings in this book were photographed and printed on photo mural paper; several others combine photography with other media. The Krusé and Deen presentation system devised for small offices that follows this discussion includes zoom lens projectors while the Bergmann presentations depend on an opaque projector.

In short, it behooves every architect to own at least one single-lens reflex camera, and with it a slide projector. Unless one wishes to go into architectural photography as a hobby or a profession, a reasonably good 35mm. camera is adequate for photographing drawings, models, and even completed buildings. An f/1.7, 50mm. standard lens has an aperture wide enough to shoot indoors under average conditions without supplementary lighting. Since most drawings and models are photographed indoors, this is an important property. A larger aperture, f/1.4, allows more flexibility, but is considerably more expensive. Be sure, however,

that the camera you buy has a removable lens, so that a 28mm. wide-angle lens fitting can be substituted for the regular lens in photographing realized buildings; this lens has a relatively short focal length. Another intermediate lens with medium focal length would be helpful in photographing models.

Newer cameras are equipped with a whole host of features not to be found in their older counterparts. Methodical types would rarely have trouble remembering to set a mechanically operated counter back to "0" upon insertion of a new film cartridge. Your author never knows whether there is film in his camera or not because he forgets to do this. On newer cameras the counter springs back to "0" automatically. There is also a movable indicator to show whether the camera is loaded with color or black and white—small things, but helpful. A much more important feature is the capacity to view the scene through the lens as it actually will appear on the film. This is made possible by a mirror mounted between the lens and the film which flips aside when the trigger is released to shoot the picture. Almost all cameras today have built-in range finders, too. Finally, almost all 35mm. cameras have triggering mechanisms to move the film forward. The only way a double exposure is possible is if you push down a button and intentionally wind the film back a frame. With newer cameras there is no need to keep supplies of clear and blue flash bulbs for indoor and outdoor use; you simply move a blue plastic sheet over the flash attachment and use clear bulbs. Flash cubes, stroboscopic lights, and other features are also common.

Modern film is available in so many different types that the rank amateur should study a manual on them and on the taking of pictures. The advice of Krusé and Deen is worth heeding: Part of the decision on choice of film should be based on laboratory facilities in a particular locality. This is important because most client slide presentations will be in color. However, for interiors it is often better to use black and white and offer actual samples of wall, floor, and fabric colors. Tri-X is so flexible in terms of ASA film speed that it offers wide possibilities of use. It used to become grainy upon enlargement to 4″ × 5″ or 8″ × 10″, but with the new version of the film, this is no longer a serious· problem. With black and white Tri-X, if you chose color that the client particularly disliked, this would not (if you'll excuse the expression) color his attitude toward the entire presentation.

An architect who never touches a drop of alcohol *might* be able to take photographs of drawings and models with the camera hand-held. Most of us require a tripod (and incidentally some older 35mm. cameras are not tapped to attach to a tripod); it is wise to acquire one which the camera can either be perched on top of (in the usual fashion) or suspended beneath. The latter capability is particularly useful for getting in close to models (architectural, of course).

For supplemental lighting some reflectors of the smaller size—10″ diameter—will be essential. Enough reflectors to supply up to 2000 watts is ample for most purposes, but this must be flexible. Drawings can be photographed with flash alone but a combination of various kinds of light—floods, spots, and others—is required for photographing models. Julius Shulman, the architectural photographer, recommends reflectors with barn doors—hinged metal visors—to control the direction of the reflected light. Many other kinds of special equipment will be needed to get into hard-to-reach openings; for example, a periscopic lens is almost essential.

The neophyte photographer should be careful not to depend too much on the light meter—built in or separate. Julius Shulman pointed out to the writer that every roll of film carries a slip with graphic depictions of the various kinds of light encountered outdoors. By using common sense and taking shots with three different lens openings—as most professionals do anyway, incidentally—the results are likely to be as good or better than those taken at the dictate of a light meter.

Many camera fans prefer a 2¼″ × 2¼″ camera to a 35mm., and it does hold some advantages—though fewer than it did a short time ago. The film size, and therefore the contact print size, is more convenient to study and to crop for enlargement. The 35mm. is so small that it is sometimes difficult to ascertain from the contact sheet, or strip, which of a series of shots should be cropped or enlarged. (It is somewhat easier to have contacts made double size than to work with an enlarging glass.) However, this is a small price to pay for the extra flexibility of the smaller size. Furthermore, a 35mm. shot (which is 7/8″ × 1 5/16″), on Plus X or Tri-X black and white, can often be enlarged by cropping to a proportion of 4″ × 5″ × 8″ or 10″ and be every bit as clear as a shot taken with a 2¼″ × 2¼″ camera. A 4″ × 5″ view camera is a delight to own, but really, like an 8″ × 10″, it is such an expensive piece of professional equipment that it should be put to rather regular use. When you become a camera bug, you will also have to have your own dark room. But even then, the best way to handle complicated photomontage is to find a professional photographer like Jack Horner. If you try this kind of project yourself (combining a site photograph with a model), the model should be shot outside at the same time of day on the same kind of day and, of course, from the same angle as the site. It is also essential that the vanishing points of the model are the same as those of the site. One way around this is to use another technique described in this chapter, which involves projecting a slide of the site on a large screen and photographing the model in front of the site. Another useful piece of equipment is a Polaroid Land camera, which has become so simple to operate that the next step in its development may very easily be the elimination of the need to push a button to expose a picture.

Slide projectors are simple to contend with (except for getting the pictures in right side up), although they, too, can be extremely complex. Many people like Carousel or cartridge projectors, and they are an advantage if a show is to be given over and over again. Slides are slipped into slots and left there more or less permanently. But for editing, or for those who need to shift slides around frequently, a stack loader is better. A stack loader is a projector into which you simply throw a series of slides in the order in which you wish to project them. Of course, as with all slide shows, it is essential that the slides be loaded so they will not only project right side up but be correctly oriented from left to right. Most presentations are made with projectors equipped with remote or automatic control. If the presentation talk is canned, it can, of course, be synchronized with the automatic projector. If you are giving your own talk, you can stand in the rear, or anywhere else for that matter, and move a little light arrow inside the projector to point out features. To some, the old-fashioned pointer holds a certain fascination, and, by using the remote control on the projector, one can stand beside the screen and indulge oneself. Even the pointer has been improved. It is now possible to obtain a retractable pocket-size metal pointer, the end of which is a ball-point pen. An architect lucky enough to have one of these could have the contract signed with the very same instrument he has used to sell the client.

The opaque projector, also known as a lazy lucy, can be very useful to the renderer or architect. Excellent ones are available from well under 100 dollars up. A projector in this low price range would be motor driven with a fan, but its image size would be limited to something like 6" × 6"; anything larger would have to be projected in sections. It is not wise to buy a projector unless the lens is optically ground and is approximately 3" to 4" in diameter. At 12-feet distance from the source, it should project an image approximately 90 inches square. A more sophisticated opaque projector

will take sections of art work up to 8½" × 11" on a sliding copy board with a 6.5 diameter f 4.5 lens. This kind of equipment will enlarge 500 percent and reduce 400 percent. It should be capable of projecting either on a drawing surface or on a wall.

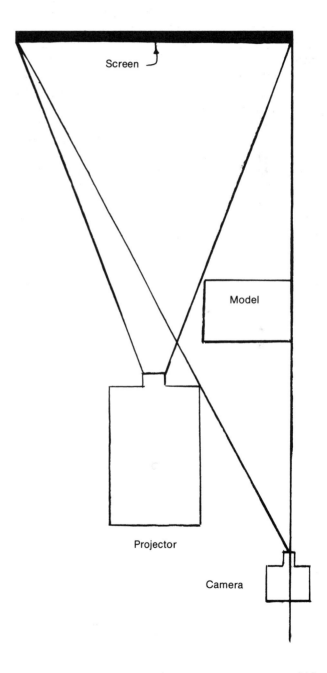

In its excellent publication, *Florida Architect*, the Florida Association of the American Institute of Architects, presented a series on small office practice to which H. Samuel Krusé, F.A.I.A., and James Deen, A.I.A., contributed an article: "Presentation Made Easy." In their discussion of tools and materials the writers said: "The really expensive tools are a camera and two projectors complete with zoom lenses. Jim's camera is a Nikon with a zoom lens, but it could be an Instamatic or any type that will take pictures for slides. A Polaroid that takes transparent pictures will work, too, if the projector is suitable."

Most architects have projectors, though not all have two with zoom lenses, and, Krusé and Deen point out, while two projectors are needed, only one need have a zoom lens. When both do, however, they say a considerable amount of "futzing" time is saved. Film choice is determined by local processing facilities. "Jim uses high-speed Ektachrome because that film can be developed locally in slides in twenty-four hours."

Before proceeding, it is necessary that a well-defined plot plan be available. Krusé and Deen describe the steps they follow in order and illustrate with some examples from one of their projects:

1. Make a simple model of the building (or of the two sides that will show in the final rendering) to the same scale as the plot plan, only slightly more carefully built than a chipboard and stick office study model, including larger details. It need not be large. It must show the mass and shape of the building and be on the same scale as the plot plan.

2. Take a roll or two of photographs of the site from various elevations and angles. If the direction of shadows has not been determined, take a series of shots at different times of day.

3. Set the model on the plot plan outside and take a roll or two of photographs of the model at approximately the same times of the day that the site shots were taken. The plot plan is, of course, oriented as the actual site lies, and remember the difference in scale in matching aspect and elevation.

4. Put site slides in one projector and model slides in the other and in a darkened room project the site on a white surface, using the zoom lens to obtain desired picture size. Select the most logical angle and elevation.

5. Project model shots over the site slide, using zoom lens to match the scale and moving the projector until the site of the model matches the shot of the actual site as closely as possible.

6. Tape a sheet of light-sensitive paper to the projection surface so that the entire image will be reproduced on it. About an hour is required to expose the lines on blueprint paper; sepia paper takes much longer.

7. If the match is exact enough, the resulting picture can be used as printed. If not, a tracing can be made using colored felt pens, pen and ink, pencil, or some other medium. If the picture is on sepia for reproduction work, it is possible to add details or make corrections directly on the first print, then reproduce as many as are needed.

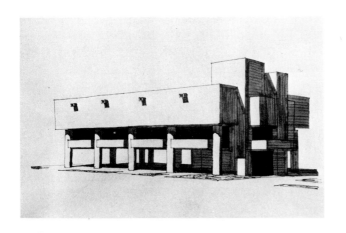

The authors continue: "In the presentation to the client, the slides of the model and the site can be shown first, leading up to the undraping of the matted, framed picture showing him exactly how his project will look on the completed site. He (the client, it might be 'they') is impressed, immediately authorizes development of the scheme into contract documents, and promptly writes the check to pay for the design development phase of the work of 'His Architect,' a really smart honcho."

**Renderers:** Robert Venturi, W. G. Clark, David Vaughan
**Architects:** Venturi and Rauch
**Hartford Stage Company** Hartford, Connecticut

The base for all three of these drawings was a photomontage made up of a photograph of a study model blown up to size and one of the actual site cut together. Mr. Clark then outlined all the forms in the photomontage in ink. Using the photograph for reference, he traced the final value rendering over the outline drawing using a Rapidograph pen. This is the first drawing that carries Henry VIII on the marquee. The one by Mr. Venturi—the second one—was executed with a felt tip pen over the same base drawing. The final version was drawn by Mr. Vaughan using much the same process Mr. Clark used.

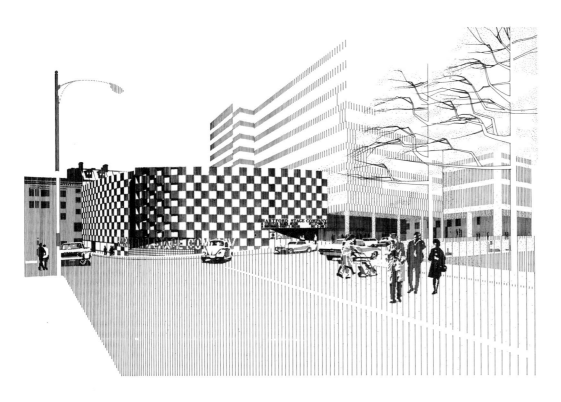

**Renderer:** Richard Bergmann
**Architect:** Richard Bergmann
**House remodeling**

Richard Bergmann uses another photographic method to avoid the time and effort involved in constructing a perspective. Here are several Polaroid camera shots of a house that was to be remodeled. One of these (the one at bottom left) is projected through an opaque projector on a piece of yellow tracing paper on the walls, where it is traced. (Please note: honesty in broadcasting makes it necessary for us to say that the rendering the architect is drawing is "pre-recorded." In other words, the projector was turned off and the lights on, and Mr. Bergmann is faking the drawing activity). At any rate, the rough perspective is moved to a board, where the finished rendering is drawn on vellum. This system makes it possible to make the rendering as large as desired. This finished drawing is on a sheet 16" × 20". The same result can be obtained by shooting a black and white (or color) slide with a 35mm. camera and using regular slide projection. The only disadvantage is that time has to be allowed to process the film before the drawing can be completed.

NEW TERMINAL FACILITIES FOR
KNICKERBOCKER AVIATION · BRIDGEPORT CONNECTICUT

**Renderers:** The Bergmann Team
**Architect:** Richard Bergmann
**New Terminal Facilities** for Knickerbocker Aviation, Bridgeport, Connecticut

A dramatic rendering came out of this Polaroid photograph of some old hangars where Corsairs were built during World War II. The original shot was enlarged and a sketch was traced over it. The new sketch included a control tower, restaurant, motel, salesroom, and, of course, parking. The drawing, in turn, was reenlarged to 10″ × 10″, the maximum Mr. Bergmann's opaque projector will take. The machine was then moved back as far as possible and a new rendering made with magic markers on a long piece of brown butcher paper 36″ wide. Different parts of the rendering were traced by members of the crew until 12 feet of paper had been consumed. Mr. Bergmann also projected photographs of aircraft cut from airplane magazines to different scales to add realism to the rendering. This new drawing, when unrolled with proper ceremony before the clients, was quite impressive, especially since the client knew the whole presentation had been completed in a very short time. The second photo shows a detail of the presentation. Mr. Bergmann uses the opaque projector as a time-saver in adding entourage because it is so simple to project trees, shrubbery, and automobiles, as well as aircraft and life, to any scale required.

**Renderer:** Ben Althen
**Architects:** Gruen Associates; McCarter, Nairne & Partners Associated Architects, Engineers, Planners
**Pacific Centre Ltd.** Vancouver, British Columbia

The base drawing for this rendering was executed in ink on vellum, 15″ × 20″. This drawing was then enlarged to 30″ × 40″ and printed on photo mural paper. Color was added, with the oil-base paints that are used to tint photographs. The color was then rubbed with cotton to give luminosity to the rendering. This process has an advantage in that the color can easily be removed if a change is necessary. The base drawing, of course, is saved for future use.

**Renderer:** Marc Nisbet
**Architect:** Skidmore, Owings & Merrill (N.Y.C.)

**Edmonton Centre** Edmonton, Alberta

The original of these renderings was approximately 19″ × 30″; their presentation size was approximately 50″ × 80″. Drawn with a Graphos pen on vellum, the final presentation was colored with felt markers. With this fine-line pen work, the shading is obviously designed to take the coloring which is added after enlargement.

**Renderer:** Marc Nisbet
**Architects:** Copeland, Noval & Israel

**Development** Dublin, Ireland

Using a similar technique as in the interiors, Marc Nisbet did this rendering 20″ × 30″ with a Graphos pen, had it enlarged to 40″ × 60″, and colored it with felt markers.

**Originator:** Bruce Cunningham-Werdnigg

The photomobiles shown here were designed by the architectural photographer Bruce Cunningham-Werdnigg. Photographs and/or drawings dry-mounted onto Styrofoam or similar lightweight panels are assembled to simulate the overall shape of the structure. Suspended by an invisible nylon thread and balanced for weight, these mobiles twirl around their vertical axis in incidental drafts. The mobiles, besides being decorative, effectively exhibit an architect's work. By judicious selection of views, graphics, lettering, and other data, any project may be shown off in this manner.

**Renderer:** Mark de Nalovy-Rozvadovski
**Architects:** Castro-Blanco, Piscioneri & Feder and Gruzen & Partners, Associated Architects
**New York State Urban Development Corporation**
106th Street, Fifth Avenue, New York, N.Y.

This extremely detailed ink rendering gives a picture so realistic that, produced with a half-tone screen as shown, it looks like a photograph.

**Originator:** George Ranalli
**Addition to New York City**

Here is a fanciful montage which, Mr. Ranalli says, uses photography as a design tool—a conceptual visualization to give form to a thought. He found a photograph of the New York skyline and then "searched for a graphic object which would communicate some sense of structure and order without getting involved in minute details. The 'addition' was a photograph of a space frame structure turned horizontally to appear to be growing out of the existing city."

He adds: "The technique here is overlapping the images so that the structure appears to fit in. The clouds and some of the existing buildings were cut so that overlapping occurs. They are placed in position and rubber-cemented together. The whole is then rephotographed."

131

**Renderer:** Yung Wang
**Architect and Planner:** Warner Burns Toan Lunde
**Harbor View of Urban Renewal Area** City of Juneau,
Alaska

This firm and its precedessors has long been known for its imaginative solution to architectural problems. The elements of this presentation are both montages. Black and white slides were taken of the harbor at Juneau. A large model was made which included solid blocks to indicate buildings that were to remain and detailed models of new buildings. The slide was enlarged on a screen to approximately 6' × 8'. The model was positioned considerably in front of the projected photograph and between the camera and the beam of the projector. The whole was rephotographed in the two views shown here.

The series of renderings of the same project were completed in three or four days, one of which was spent collecting appropriate photographs from old magazines to use in the montages.* In some cases, the photograph determined the perspective for the drawing, as with the skating rink (Rendering 1) whose trussed roof structure came from a two-page spread in *Fortune* magazine. This photograph dictated the size of the drawing as well as the perspective for the surrounding shopping center. Only a few photographs of people, clipped from magazines, were used; the rest were drawn in. The same thing happened in Rendering 2. Good photos of a school bus, a traffic light, snow-removal activity, and some unposed-looking figures provided an excellent foreground for the shopping center.

1

2

*Mr. Wang is one of the first people this writer has heard saying he missed *Life* and *Look*. They were the *only* sources for large numbers of clippings of photographs of plain people behaving routinely. If renderers of the world will only unite, we may get *Life* back.

3

4

In Rendering 3, again, a couple of fortuitous photographs provided the raison d'etre for the drawing and dictated, also, the perspective lines. In Rendering 4 the idea was to take advantage of the actual dock area at Juneau, to show a ship which might have arrived from San Francisco or Seattle and the excitement and activity attendant on such an event. The renderer found some photographs of Eskimos as well as some tourist-looking types to occupy his rendering, which consists of nothing more than an oversized trellis structure, a couple of small buildings in the background, some signs, and two rather imposing totems. In Rendering 5 the renderer shows how some of Warner Burns Toan Lunde Townland Housing System prefabs would straddle a highway filled with real cars. Heaven help anyone falling from a balcony onto 55mph traffic! But to give the renderer his due, it would have been difficult these days to locate a highway photograph with 35mph speed-limit signs. In Rendering 6 the perspective was constructed first and appropriate entourage pasted on top of it. The renderer points to the sky, where three separate pieces of sky were joined because a large enough single piece could not be found. The original intention had been to produce only two renderings of this project, but the team got carried away and came up with several. Such renderings are not for presentation to the client, but when photographed and projected they make a creditable presentation.

5

6

The renderer makes the point that, to be effective, work of this kind must be spontaneous. One either finds the most important object and uses that to establish the mood of the illustration or, if it is a building or complex, one lays out the perspective rough and then finds appropriate entourage which one mounts on a piece of tracing paper covering the original perspective. The rendering is then completed with magic markers. In large offices where work is billed on a cost-plus basis, infinite pains can be exercised to produce exquisite drawings. But today even large firms seek to simplify the presentation process. After all, a presentation that may have taken three months to produce will be viewed by the client in an hour or so. For this reason WBTL, like other busy offices, attempts to show the best of everything, playing down details and producing whatever is necessary to effect a mood.

WBTL has also done impressive drawings, up to 30 feet long, but it is too difficult to get any notion of what they are like on pages this size. Their production method, however, is rather simple and can best be explained in words. A particular project was the Tri-State School for the mentally retarded in Albany, New York. It was to be on a hilly site somewhat like an Italian hill-town. The housing units were basically the same. An elevation with lots of shadows was drawn as the basic building. The site was then drawn on the thirty-foot-long piece of tracing paper. Autopositives were produced of the basic rendering in four different exposures. These were mounted on the back of the site elevation with the darkest units in the front. Those farthest back were the lightest and, of course, the two other degrees of exposures were for units in between. Autopositive prints are ideal for this kind of presentation because, like sepia, they can be erased. This was important because trees had to be drawn in the foreground and background to add realism to the whole.

Somewhat the same procedure can be followed in erecting a tall building in which all the floors except the top and bottom are to be alike. An elevation is made of one floor, and autopositives are made from this. These are then mounted carefully on tracing paper and a new autopositive is made to which top and bottom floors may be added. This is similar to the process used by Rex Allen Associates for interstitial floors in hospitals. (See p. 93.)

A more realistic method of doing the same thing is to make a detailed model of one floor and take photographic shots of it from whatever viewpoint you choose, changing the camera angle as you proceed, to provide proper perspective. Photographs of similarly detailed models, of the top and bottom floors can be substituted at the appropriate time. Thus your film strip can be developed into a 20-, 30-, 40-, or 100-story building.

**Photographer:** Jack Horner, Pennyroyal
Productions
**Renderer:** Marc Nisbet
**Architects:** Skidmore, Owings & Merrill

**New York Hospital** East River Front, New York

The photographer took a series of aerial shots of the site from a helicopter. This one shows the entire site with all of the new buildings rendered in place by Marc Nisbet. However, this single shot represents a very small segment of the entire cooperative project, which involved not only the renderer and photographer but various partners and staff members from the architects' office. This team produced an extraordinary slide presentation that has to be seen to be appreciated. However, an explanation of how it was accomplished and the results may be useful. Before proceeding, it must be explained that several experimental processes had to be gone through before a final scenario could be prepared.

Despite its complexity this project had to be completed quickly. Mr. Nisbet started with a 30" × 38" print. He rendered the buildings on yellow tracing paper. This tracing remained in place over the photograph and was, in turn, covered with a clear, prepared acetate overlay. Film thus prepared will accept a spray wash tempera or any opaque or transparent water-base paint. The white paint representing the floors in the photograph was painted on the face of the acetate, which was then turned over and painted with a dark color to mask out the old buildings which showed through on the photograph.

The slide show, which was in color, was designed to show the removal of one existing building at a time. Each building to be removed was outlined in dark brown with an opaque Bourges transfer sheet. These were then covered with the proposed new structure in each case. Since the hospital is to operate all the while the buildings are being erected, there are ten steps of this kind before the entire new complex is complete.

The photographic job was a very tricky one and Mr. Horner not only took six or eight shots of each slide using different f stops, but he took two rolls for each set of photographs to be sure there was a back-up set. Besides this, he bought all the film in one lot so there would be no possibility of variation in color or anything else. The camera and the original photograph were then set in position and never moved. Cutouts of each of the rendered buildings were applied to the photograph with an adhesive sprayed on the back of the art. This provided just enough tension to hold it in place. The final time around the procedure was reversed. The entire drawing was mounted in place, as shown in this photograph, and then each building was cut off and removed until the first building to be added remained. It was then, of course, shown in reverse as though the buildings were being added.

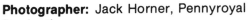

**Photographer:** Jack Horner, Pennyroyal Productions
**Architects:** Skidmore, Owings & Merrill

**Olympic Tower** Fifth Avenue at 51st Street, New York, New York

Even more convincing, in some ways, than a model, a rendering, or even a slide show, are three-dimensional photographs of a model, especially in color. The original 35mm. slides from which these reproductions were made are in color. The distance between the eyes is 2¼" and the photographs reproduced side by side here (with the one for the left eye at left and vice versa) are 2¼" apart center to center. It is possible for most people to force their eyes to bring one image over the other. This is accomplished by taking a piece of black board approximately 5" to 6" wide by 7¼" high and placing it exactly between the two photographs. You then bring your head down toward the page so that the edge of the board is exactly in the center of the nose and the left eye views the left photo and the right eye the right photo. By concentrating, it is possible to bring these images together to provide a three-dimensional picture of the lobby of the Olympic Tower.

This photograph, taken with south light, is cloudless. All the details of Saks Fifth Avenue to the immediate right and St. Patrick's Cathedral beyond it are clearly evident.

From exactly the same viewpoint, on a different day, Mr. Horner shot for clouds only; note also the flag at left which was not present in the first shot. The photographer burned all of the buildings out of this negative and transferred the sky in his original photo. The drawings were rendered on clear acetate film and the negatives were glued together with a clear spray adhesive.

**Photographer:** Jack Horner, Pennyroyal Productions
**Renderer:** Marc Nisbet
**Architects:** Skidmore, Owings & Merrill

**Olympic Tower** Fifth Avenue and 51st Street New York, New York

Jack Horner and Marc Nisbet have worked together closely on many projects. This one is primarily a photographic project, but Marc Nisbet's touching-up was essential to make the final photograph convincing.

The purpose of this project was to show the client, Aristotle Onassis, how his new building would look with a mirrored facade. The architect's model implied a bronze frame and bronze-tinted windows. The captions follow the step-by-step progression. A remarkable aspect of this project is that it was all done on an extremely tight schedule. The renderer did all of this touch-up work in watercolor with various-sized brushes.

This shot shows the rather detailed ½" scale model of St. Patrick's Cathedral in front of the bronze model of the proposed Olympic Tower.

A large sheet of white board was carefully curved to change the apparent color of the model. To the right may be seen a table covered with the various crushed material used to reflect clouds and shadows onto the facade of the model. It was essential to take this shot from an angle in order to match exactly the perspective of the site shot.

The finished photograph. Mr. Horner made two prints, 30" × 38". He physically cut out the photograph of the Olympic Tower and glued it to the site shot. In the process he covered foliage off the trees in the left-hand foreground and disturbed the connection between the bottom of the model photo and the cars and pedestrians in the original site photograph. In transforming bronze to mirror, the west facade of the new building had been washed out. Also, the mirrored reflection of the Cathedral spire in the model was not fully detailed. At this point, Mr. Nisbet touched up the combination print with ink and opaque washes. It is necessary to wet the area thoroughly before attempting to paint on it. The renderer used a fine brush for the verticals and horizontals on the building's west elevation and added quatrefoils and other ornamentation to the reflected spire, spotted in the foliage which had been cut out of the original print, added some heads and car tops in front of the new building, and improved the flag in the left foreground.

**Renderer:** John S. Walling
**Architects:** Wolff-Zimmer-Gunsul-Fasca-Ritter
**Headquarters for Portland General Electric** Portland, Oregon

Mr. Walling's technique is quite individual. His original drawing is usually small, 10″ × 12″ or 15″ × 18″. Often he does it on a piece of fairly smooth paper toweling—a material about which he says, "You'll have to admit that the capital outlay for drawing paper is quite small." However, if the paper toweling is not large enough to produce the necessary detail, he will (dare I say) throw caution to the wind and use rough watercolor paper. His original drawing is executed with various types of black marking pens—some fresh for the line technique and some practically dry for shading and tones.

The next step takes him to an offset printer, where he orders a same-size photographic negative with a 133 line screen. This negative is enlarged and printed, usually about twice the original size on a mural photostatic paper with a slight tooth. A section from the screened negative of the Portland General Electric headquarters is reproduced here as an example. The black and white version is reproduced for newspaper publicity. When used for display, color is applied with a combination of marking pens and oil pastels. The original is mounted on Styrofoam board and under Plexiglas.

Slides are made, also; in this case, the entire rendering and two enlargements are shown of sections of the original colored drawing, reproduced here in black and white. These are used in a slide presentation.

The renderer says that while this looks and sounds complicated, it actually is quite fast compared to pencil or conventional ink. Its disadvantage lies in the fact that the perspective must be laid directly on the towel or watercolor paper, which is more difficult than the usual method of making a transfer.

# 8. OTHER PRESENTATIONS

## THE CLIENT AND PUBLICITY

Attempts are constantly being made to a) simplify the process of making a presentation; b) make presentations more comprehensible to the client even if the process became more complicated; c) train the client to understand simple presentations—that is, teach him to "see" and "draw back" to you; d) devise methods to obfuscate the project or, at least, the parts of which the architect wishes to have open options, such as design details, for example; or form combinations of a and b, or a and d.

Most presentations are meant to show a client how his building or project will look when it is built. There may be a certain element of danger involved in trying to teach a client really to *see*, but the benefits would probably outweigh the peril. At any rate, for what they are worth, here are some pointers that may be of some use.

A few years ago the author of this book produced a paper on education. In it he advocated a complete change in early education from present subject-oriented programs to what he called tool schools in which children, at their own rate, would be taught, among other things, tactile and muscular control, how to walk and to dance, what muscles come into play in the performance of various sports, how to read, write, and do sums, how to read music, and how to draw. He was not suggesting that everyone should become an athlete, dancer, actor, musician, artist, or architect, but that everyone learn the basics required to live a full, comfortable life as well as those required for any vocational or avocational pursuit he might wish to follow.

But, alas, such schools are probably not practical. Meanwhile, however, one might think that abstract patterns, partial images, melds, jumping and twisting letters, and words used in TV programs and commercials might lead people in general to understand better two-dimensional architectural drawings. But, for some reason, people do not "see" a good many things at all. They may call a building a glass box, but if asked to make a drawing of it, the vast majority would shrug off such a possibility with, "I can't draw a straight line."

The client who has difficulty describing something he has seen, or, perhaps, only imagined, can be educated rather easily to the realization that he can draw a straight line or a curved line and, in fact, that he probably does so many times a day. The late Edward H. Freedman—an artist and Renaissance man—developed a method of which he

says (and rightly so) that a ten-minute trial will convince anyone he *can* draw. He has set forth his method in a modest paperback book *How to Draw*, subtitled, *If you can write, you can draw*. In his introduction, he says that he is teaching "conversational drawing," not art. He goes on to say that what he really is teaching is how to see. But let him explain his method:

He shows how many everyday objects are essentially cylinders—cans, cigarettes, lipsticks, glasses, and the like.

He also describes how to use "ones" to make boxes.*

The lines which form the opposite sides of the rectangle are approximately parallel. These straight lines should be as easily drawn as you write "ones"—without hesitation. Do the longer lines first, and then cross them with the two shorter lines. Do them quickly so that your lines will look firm. The lines in each set should be of equal length, respectively.

The next point to develop is the height of the box. This is determined by drawing a straight line, down, at the front corner, the one converging toward you. Make a mark on this line which will determine the desired height of the box. Bear in mind that in this lesson you are drawing the box from the top down.

Practice this lesson at great length until you are able to draw a box as easily as you write the word "box."

—IF YOU CAN *write* 1100

—YOU CAN *write* A CYLINDER

Begin by *Writing* two zeros far apart

join them with two "ones" like this

add the ashes and smoke.

Start with the top of the box—it's a rectangle which determines the width and depth of the box.

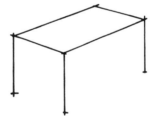

Then draw similar lines of the same length at the left and right corners.

To complete the box, join the ends of the straight lines, and add some light tone on the front, and a darker tone on the side, leaving the top white.

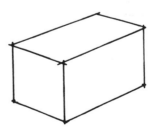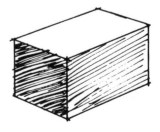

*Reproduced by permission of Bantam Books Inc.

If you present a copy of this book to your client—or tell him where to buy it—and he reads it, he will soon discover that he not only can draw straight and curved lines but he can draw almost anything imaginable from a glass box to the most sophisticated objects, like furniture, automobiles, or typewriters. He might even be able to make a creditable drawing of something he has seen but has difficulty describing verbally.

Once a presentation has been made and the project definitely given the go-ahead, it is usually desirable to let the press in on the story. If the client retains a public relations firm, the architect should get to know the people in it. If the architect has his own public relations firm or department, it should coordinate the architect's publicity with the client's.

When public relation wires are clear, it should be possible to avoid seeing your work reproduced as, for example, "an artist's sketch of the new Ray Goulding Building." Artists' and architects' sketches still appear so labeled in as good a newspaper as *The New York Times*. The best way to avoid this treatment is to cement your own credit line on all photographs of your presentations, which should read: "not to be reproduced without a credit line," followed by your firm name. If you want to be really sweet, you might even insist that it also say: "Architectural rendering by Olympia Eggleston," assuming, of course, that she was your renderer.

Presentation material to be published should be chosen carefully. Generally speaking, most news media will get better results with art copy that is contrasty because the screen is coarse. A newspaper still printed by letterpress will use a 50 line screen, but many newer newspapers are printed by offset and reproduce art with a 100 line screen. Paper has become so expensive, however, that even slick magazines often are forced to reproduce with a 110 line screen. In books such as this one, however, on high-quality offset paper, 220 line or finer screens are used. The same rendering is reproduced here in 100, 120 133, and 150 line screen. A contrasty subject was chosen intentionally. The rendering of Summit Towers in Guttenberg, New Jersey, is by Baehr for Gruzen & Partners, Architects.

144

## ADJACENT PROJECTS

It is always rewarding when an architectural firm is able to design two adjacent projects. This happy situation befell Gruzen & Partners, who designed both the New York Police Headquarters and the Foley Square Courthouse Annex. The photographs of the models are shown for orientation. One is a view of the Police Headquarters showing the parking garage and the pedestrian plaza; the other, a photo by Louis Checkman, shows the Police Headquarters at left and the Foley Square Courthouse Annex at right.

The renderings are in the distinctive styles of their delineators. The one with the Police Headquarters farthest back is by Mark de Nalovy-Rozvadovski. The two that bring us up close to the building are, of course, by Helmut Jacoby.

The two renderings of the Courthouse Annex are by E. Burden. The second rendering has more cars, people, and trees. The surrounding buildings, also, are more fully delineated, giving the entire rendering a greater sense of reality.

Gruzen & Partners use traditional (and excellent) renderings, such as those shown here, as well as models. However, they are working also with slide shows made up of 2¼″ × 2¼″ slides that are shot continuously from site visits and conceptualization to design and through construction to final use.

Renderings such as those shown here are usually 20″ × 30″ or 30″ × 40″ and are drawn over mechanically constructed perspectives. Sometimes Mylar is used, but illustration board is often used when the rendering is designed for public display.

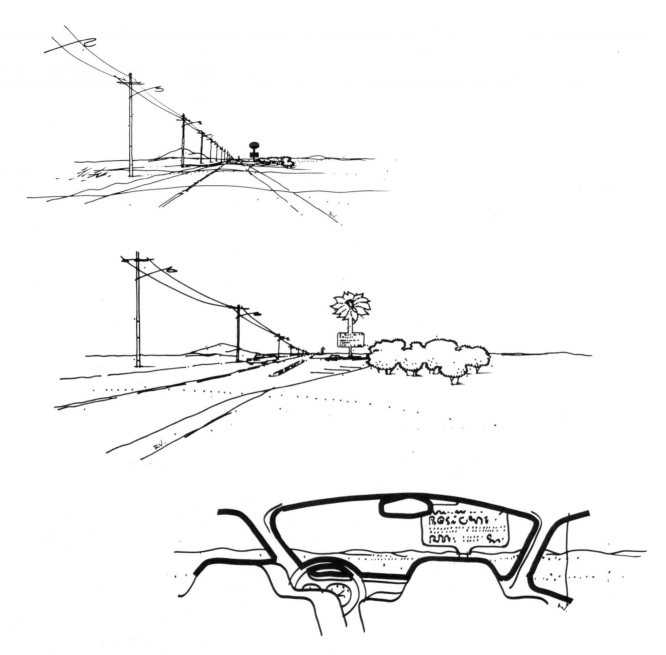

**Renderer:** Robert Venturi
**Architects:** Venturi and Rauch
**20 Mule Team Parkway** California City, California

These ink sketches were drawn with a flair pen to show how signs work on a high-speed highway.

The distant view would show the sign in silhouette; by middle distance the flower would be recognized; and when the time came to pull over, the lettering would be legible through the windshield while the flower would be hidden.

The particular sign is for a public area called Borax Bill Park. For the curious, the sign reads: "The 20 mule teams on their trips from Death Valley to Mojave would cover about 16 miles daily camping each night in the desert. This picnic area is named in honor of one of the most famous drivers, William Parkinson, better known as 'Borax Bill.'" The flower is an orchid cactus. The other flowers are, left to right, the globe cactus, hatchet catcus, and hedgehog catcus.

The Mojave aster is used in a sign designed for the approach to Galileo Hill, and as you approach the first community, there appears, of course, an advertising sign for the California City Holiday Inn.

**Renderer:** Mark Ueland
**Architects:** Ueland and Junker
**1. Scheme for a Shopping Mall**
**2. Penn's Landing** Philadelphia

The rendering of the shopping mall was executed on black scratch board, approximately 20″ × 30″, with a metal stylus. This method was chosen be- cause it is a good one to use to study lighting. Renderings in different media may also be used effectively in negative. A black and white and also a negative version of Mr. Ueland's pencil rendering of Penn's Landing are shown here as a contrast to the white on black scratch board rendering of the shopping mall. The original drawing, on white tracing paper, was approximately 12″ × 18″.

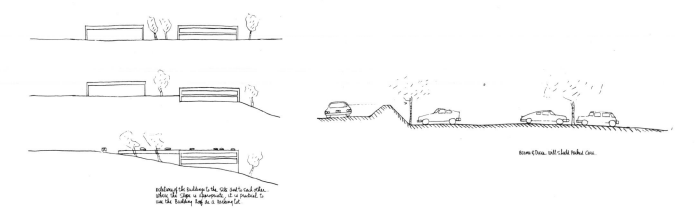

relation of the Buildings to the Site and to each other.
Where the slope is appropriate, it is practical to
use the Building Roof as a Parking Lot.

Berms & Trees will shield Parked Cars.

**Renderer:** James Morrison Leefe
**Architects and Engineers:** Giffels Associates, Inc.

Two presentations follow by the architects and engineering firm Giffels Associates, Inc. The first is for a Research and Development Center for General Electric in Twinsburg, Ohio. Having started from scratch on a virgin 209.7 acre site, it will eventually contain nine building complexes with a construction program that will probably extend over a period of twenty years. The architects took innumerable photographs of the site from the ground and from the air. They wanted to be certain that the new industrial complex would relate as pleasantly as possible to its rural neighbors.

James Morrison Leefe, who is Director of Design of Giffels Associates, believes that all presentations are intimately associated with the design process. He also believes that the presentation must be individually tailored to the corporate structure. Client contact on projects of this magnitude operate on three levels:

1. Work sessions with the day-to-day working group.
2. Presentation and work sessions at middle-management level.
3. Formal presentations to top-level management and the board of directors.

The material shown here is used for all three of these levels, but frequently it is severely edited and made more formal by the addition of a presentation model or renderings prepared by an outside renderer for top-level consumption.

Clients in general do not particularly like to be sold a solution. They like to know how a project evolved and what alternatives were considered, which is why early studies, diagrams, and any other devices the architects can think of, are included in Giffels' presentations.

All drawings in this presentation were the work of James Leffe alone.

Since the site at the Development Center ranged from flat to rolling countryside, three schemes relating buildings to the site were roughed in in the first drawing. Possible solutions to the ever-present parking problem are shown in the second sketch. Note the extreme simplicity of the trees and the unidentifiable characteristics of the automobiles. Thus, in a project of this kind, which will take several years to complete, the automobiles will never look dated. An additional virtue of such simplicity is that less drawing time is required. The client was quite capable of understanding rough sketches of this kind.

A most important requirement in this laboratory is flexibility of electrical and other services. The drawings present different ways of integrating them in a variety of structural systems which will provide orderly control of all the spaghetti overhead while still allowing freedom to set up experiments.

152

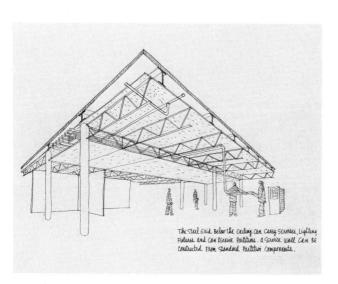

The Steel Grid Below the Ceiling Can Carry Services, Lighting Fixtures and Can Receive Partitions. a Service Wall Can Be Constructed From Standard Partition Components.

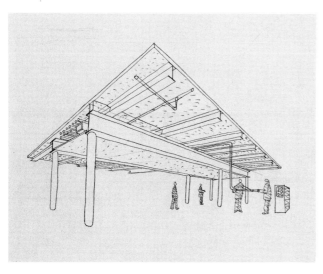

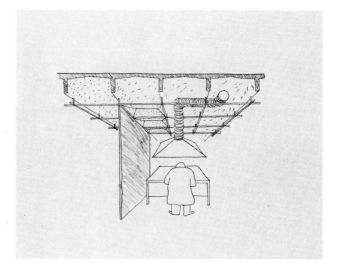

Four drawings show the architect's exploration of the building concept. Since the last buildings might be built twenty years from now, the architect wanted his client to consider buildings which would live well in the present and lead to the unknown future. A very rough sketch from James Leefe's notebook is included to show his initial response after the first building had been programmed. In the color section a much more detailed—but still, by most standards, not a finished—rendering is shown.

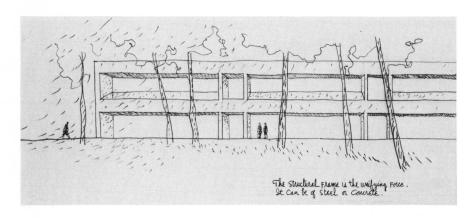

The structural frame is the unifying force. It can be of steel or concrete.

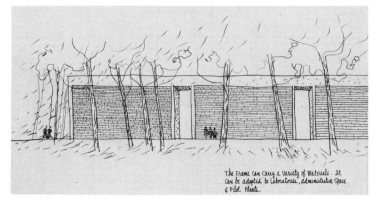

The frame can carry a variety of materials. It can be adapted to laboratories, administrative space & pilot plants.

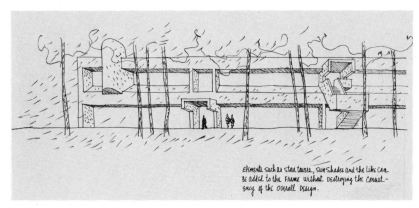

Elements such as stairtowers, sunshades and the like can be added to the frame without destroying the consistency of the overall design.

using the structural bay as a Building Block, it is possible to tailor Buildings to the configurations of the site.

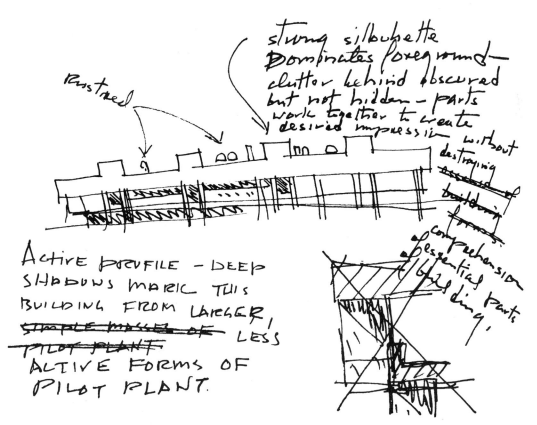

Rustred

strong silhouette
Dominates foreground—
clutter behind obscured
but not hidden — parts
work together to create
desired impression without
destroying
building
forms:
comprehension
of essential parts
of building.

Active profile — deep
shadows mark this
building from larger,
~~simple masses of~~ less
~~pilot plant~~
active forms of
pilot plant.

The second project by Giffels Associates is the future headquarters of the Michigan Branch of the American Automobile Association and the Detroit Inter-Insurance Company. It is on a thirty-acre site in a community developed by the Ford Motor Company outside Dearborn, called Fairlane. James Leefe was also the rendered for this presentation.

Like the one for General Electric, this presentation is made up of several parts. Whenever possible, a slide show is presented. James Leefe likes, if possible, to accompany the slide show with key drawings hung from the wall. Many conference rooms lack facilities for hanging drawings, and, of course, slides help resolve that limitation. Giffels's presentations also include brochures with key drawings, text, and facts and figures.

The rough sketch of the 350,000 square foot, three-story office building is shown, and then two photographs of the model and two renderings of details. The model used in this presentation was a crude cardboard one made in the course of developing the design. When the time came to make the presentation, Mr. Leefe went to the corner art supply store for some acrylic paint and spent the Saturday before presentation day painting the cardboard.

Like many large firms, Giffels Associates has a skilled model maker who works in a fully-equipped shop. However, detailed models are only made when requested by the client and then at extra cost.

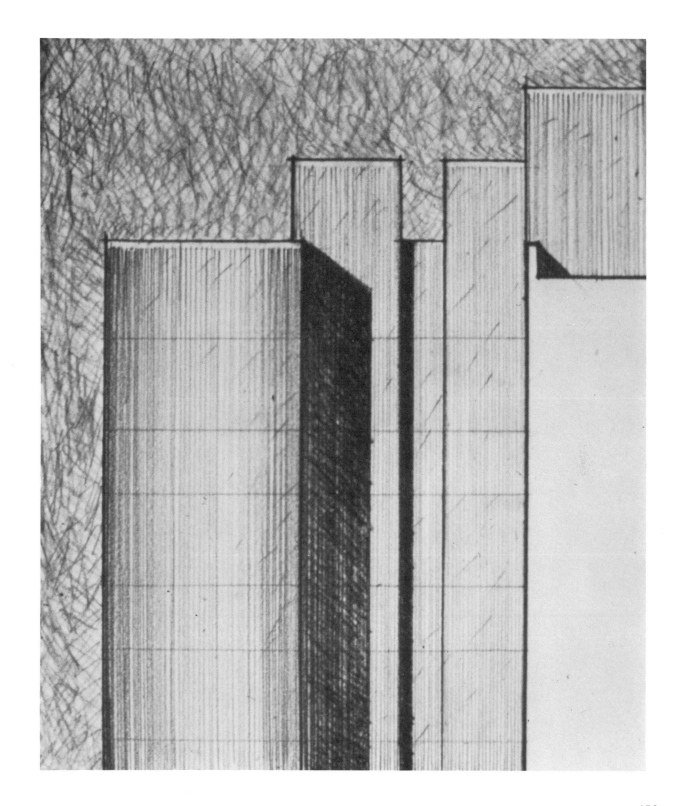

159

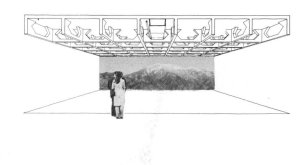

**Renderer:** James Morrison Leefe
**Architects:** Leefe & Ehrenkrantz
**Immaculate Heart College**

The first words of the client for this school were: "Don't box us into fixed classrooms." To give the client an idea of what the space would look like, Mr. Leefe made a drawing of the basic structure in one-point perspective. He then cut out the wall to the rear of the space and mounted the rendering over a photograph of a mountain taken from an aerial photograph overlooking the site. The aerial photograph of the site is shown first, and next the one-point perspective superimposed over a section of the photograph to dramatize the view through the glass wall. This shows the space convincingly. The collage in the third illustration is mounted on the basic structural drawing and suggests how the space might be arranged and occupied by the people in the college using their own art and other materials as they see fit.

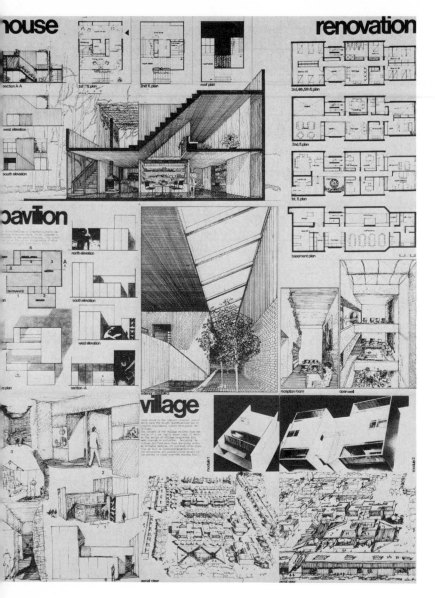

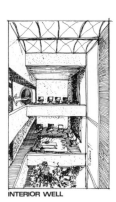

**RECEPTION AREA**     **INTERIOR WELL**

**Architect and renderer:** Shung M. Louie

A simple and effective brochure for the small office can be reproduced on blueprint paper. The final sheet shown here, opened out, is 28½″ × 33″, but it folds down to 8½″ × 11″, a size easily mailed, handled, *and* filed. The presentation is made up of drawings to illustrate Mr. Louie's design talent as well as his ability as a "presentation man," to use his term. (A rendering done by Mr. Louie for Welton

Becket Associates appears on page 77.) The method used to combine photographs with drawings was to mount both on a piece of illustration board. The entire board was then photographed and a Chromoflex print made of it. Such a print is a positive print on acetate film which can be fed through a diazo machine for inexpensive reproductions in sepia or some other color. Details from the brochure are shown.

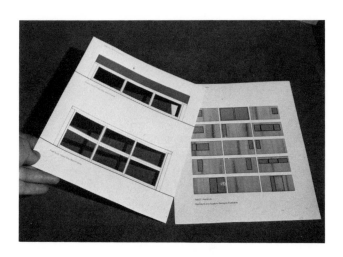

**Source:** Omega Structures Stamford, Connecticut

A simple but effective method for demonstrating the flexibility of Omega's pre-finished components is illustrated here. It is actually an enclosure in a brochure describing the Kistler system. On each side of a solid card are printed various standard inset panels positioned so that a die-cut card can be placed over them. The die-cut panel has printed on one side a one-story version with a hip roof and a two-story version with a gable roof. The other side is a one-story version with a gable roof and a two-story version with a flat roof. By shifting the two cards around, one gets a fairly clear idea of how a house built using this sytem would look on the exterior.

# 9. THE PRINT MEDIUM— DETROIT 1990

The Plan Commission of the City of Detroit began work on Detroit 1990/An Urban Design Concept for the Inner City, in 1963. Charles Blessing, Director of City Planning for the City of Detroit, had talked with large numbers of people about every aspect of the problems confronting the inner city. He had asked their advice and explained that it was possible to fulfill their needs and expectations.

No flashy image-making presentation, the result— a set of seven brochures and a large folded map all shown in the photo—is instead an excellent use of the print medium. Some of the parts of the presentation are photographic; others are drawings in pencil or ink. The same photograph or drawing is used more than once in different guises, depending on the part of the brochure in which it appears. The drawings themselves, all the work of architects, are used imaginatively, and the text is concise and understandable. Nor is it in a typeface so small that anyone over twenty-four and a half years old would have to use a magnifying glass to read it. It is altogether a creditable presentation. From the point of view of graphic design, it is interesting to compare the credits of the introductory book, reproduced here, with the letterhead of

the City of Detroit, also shown. The latter looks as though it might have been designed (for free) by a printer in the depths of the Great Depression.

The introductory sixty-page book explains that the presentation is in two parts: structure or "concept" and content or "design." While some indication of the appearance of future buildings is included—indeed necessary—things are not gelled into a mold. This is, after all, a concept into which architecture not yet dreamt about will ultimately be realized. Another recurrent theme in this concept is that its explicitness will permit modification as required by the citizens themselves in the years to come.

In the Introduction, Ralph Warburton sums up the presentation's impact by pointing out that it makes analogies to both the modern and historic planning of other cities.

The following pages consist of selected excerpts and illustrations taken rather freely out of context from the brochures. Text selections are included with the art and the technical information about it, as though they, too, were illustrations, the better to impart the flavor of the entire presentation.

The Detroit City Plan presentation consists of a map, 36″ square, printed in green and sepia. When the two are laid one over the other a third color, a deep brown, results. Seven 12″ × 12″ brochures, printed in one to four flat colors make up the balance of the presentation. Usually not more than one or two colors are used at a time; thus when additional colors are employed, their dramatic effect is that much greater. The whole was boxed.

## CITY OF DETROIT

MAYOR / Roman S. Gribbs

CITY CLERK / George C. Edwards

CITY TREASURER / Robert J. Temple

COMMON COUNCIL / Mel Ravitz, President, Ernest C. Browne, Jr., David Eberhard, Nicholas Hood, Carl Levin, William C. Rogell, Robert Tindal, Anthony Wierzbicki, Philip J. Van Antwerp

CITY PLAN COMMISSION / Acting President, Eldon K. Andrews, Irwin I. Cohn, Elihu Geer, Jack L. Korb, Amedeo Leone, F. P. Rhoades, Joseph W. Williams

DIRECTOR OF CITY PLANNING / Charles A. Blessing

URBAN DESIGN STUDY TEAM UNDER THE DIRECTION OF CHARLES A. BLESSING: Charles T. McCafferty, planner in charge, Charles T. Harris, S. Kenneth Neumann, Michael Southworth, Wirachai Wongpanit, David M. Trigiani, Alan Melting

Noel Copeland, Glen Small, Tod Williams, Lydia Kytasty, Jerome F. Gibbons

BROCHURE CONCEPTION AND DESIGN / Alan Melting, Michael Southworth

BROCHURE TEXT / Noel Copeland, Alan Melting

The publication of this report was made possible through an Urban Renewal Demonstration Grant awarded by the Department of Housing and Urban Development, under the provisions of Section 314 of the Housing Act of 1954, as amended, to the Detroit City Plan Commission.

OFFICERS
Jack L. Korb
*President*

Charles R. Scales, Jr.
*Vice President*

Charles A. Blessing
*Director of City Planning*

Carl W. Almblad
*Acting Assistant Director*

## City of Detroit

Roman S. Gribbs, *Mayor*

OFFICE OF

CITY PLAN COMMISSION

8th Floor City-County Building

Two Woodward Avenue

Detroit, Michigan 48226

Telephone 224-3500

COMMISSIONERS
Eldon K. Andrews
Irwin I. Cohn
Elihu Geer
Jack L. Korb
Amedeo Leone
Tibor Payzs
F. P. Rhoades, M.D.
Charles R. Scales, Jr.
Joseph W. Williams

Letterhead of the City of Detroit.

Credit page of introductory brochure.

*Night Shot of Detroit Present.* A dramatic use of photography produced on a spread in the introductory brochure, this shot was printed from a high-contrast negative from a photograph taken by architect Alan Melting. It shows the radial streets of Detroit that converge on the Central Business District.

This exploration into the future of Detroit follows from the belief that we will not have a chosen future if we do not think about it. The presentation of Detroit 1990 is not of the Detroit that will be, but rather one of many alternatives that might be ...

Many assumptions are implicit in this proposal. We will make explicit only three. First, that the automobile and similar forms of mass transit will be dominant for the next 20 years. This should not imply that other systems ranging from subway to minirail should not be considered and prototypes built. It is only through making alternatives visible that we can build for the 30 years ahead. We assume that leisure time will increase for the citizen, and we attempt to accommodate this through concept and design, ranging from imaginative use of existing potential open space

anticipating innovative social programs and providing centers to house them. These include small neighborhood parks, Community Colleges, etc. Our final assumption, the most basic and crucial, is that the process of change will continue within the Inner City for the next 30 years ...

[Detroit] ... has inherent potentials upon which to build. The [Detroit] River exists as a reason for the city to be and much of the city is spiritually, if not physically, oriented to it. The riverfront, its ports bustling with sweeping cranes and ships from around the world, could rival those of Hamburg, Marseilles, Rotterdam. The radial pattern of the major streets converging on the Central Business District is an indication of where the heart of Detroit lies and has the potential of relieving the monotonous grid covering most of the city...

*Inner City—Form Concept.* Architect Michael Southworth drew this with a china marking pencil on vellum. The original, 12" × 12", was reproduced full size in the introductory brochure.

The design proposes to reinforce three imageable districts—the Central Business District, Corridor, and New Center—and to create three new districts—East and West City and the Riverfront . . .

The resources and mixture of activities in the Woodward Corridor, the residential build-up of East City around the linera open space of Forest Park, the forms and spaces of the West City oriented toward the community shopping center, the impact of a revitalized Central Business District, the prototype for the growing New Center area and the water orientation of the Riverfront shape the image of the content of the Inner City.

*Key Map and Greenway Perspective of Detroit Inner City.* This map was drawn by architect Charles Harris in India ink on vellum. The original was 24" × 36". It is used throughout the presentation in different ways. It first appears in the introductory presentation in negative with key numbers identifying the principal sections of the city.

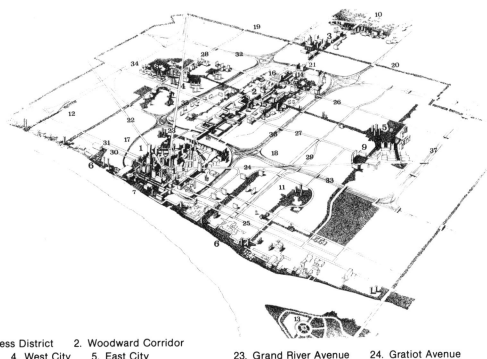

Key:

| | |
|---|---|
| 1. Central Business District | 2. Woodward Corridor |
| 3. New Center    4. West City    5. East City | |
| 6. Riverfront    7. Civic Center    8. University Park | |
| 9. Forest Park    10. Woodward Park    11. Elmwood Park | |
| 12. Gateway Park    13. Belle Isle    14. Cultural Center | |
| 15. Medical Center    16. Wayne State University | |
| 17. West Side Industrial    18. Eastern Market. | |
| 19. West Grand Boulevard    20. East Grand Boulevard | |
| 21. Woodward Avenue    22. Michigan Avenue | |

| | |
|---|---|
| 23. Grand River Avenue | 24. Gratiot Avenue |
| 25. Jefferson Avenue | 26. Warren Avenue |
| 27. Mack Boulevard | 28. Twelfth Boulevard |
| 29. St. Aubin Boulevard | 30. Fort Street |
| 31. Lafayette Boulevard | 32. Ford Expressway |
| 33. Fisher Expressway | 34. Jeffries Expressway |
| 35. Lodge Expressway | 36. Chrysler Expressway |
| 37. Mt. Elliot Expressway | |

The enclosing, leading spaces of the core area [Central Business District] are a result of the Woodward Plan of 1806. Inspired by the L'Enfant Plan of Washington, D.C., the "Governor and Judges Plan" plotted the city in a hexagonal pattern with great circuses every 4,000 feet along diagonals, with rectangular spaces at intermediate points. While the plan was soon abandoned, the excitement of diagonals and irregular block patterns of the Central Business District is a part of the rich and imageable legacy left us by the pattern.

The vehicular sequence down Woodward Avenue is made up of a number of events. One passes through the great expanses of the large park to the north of New Center, approaching the wall of form comprising the New Center. Upon entering New Center one is compressed by the man-made form and a literal gateway is created into the Corridor. The subtle curve of Woodward Avenue briefly conceals the form goal of the Central Business District and then reveals it again, larger and more immediate. More bridges occur along this well-defined route, creating a rhythm of light and shadow to counterpoint the flashing glimpses of activity, and then one finally bursts upon Grand Circus Park, being immersed in the Central Business District form, becoming part of it and involved with it.

This sequence is reversible though less dramatic, and the New Center gateway announces to one and all that one is leaving the stimulation and humanly oriented Inner City.

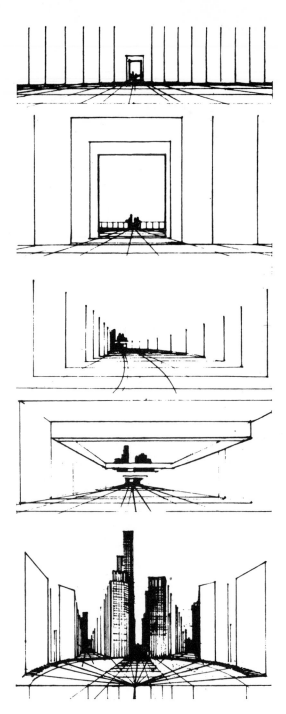

*Sequence—New Center to Circus Park.* The originals of these drawings, which were drawn on vellum, 4½" × 12", are by Architect Noel Copeland. In the introductory brochure, they are reproduced in sepia negative.

Along the way passing varying plants and forms, the park can unfold a study of natural things, varieties, growth and decay... Floor surfaces can vary: soft grasses, rocky pavement, sand, to lead the way, to reflect the mood of the space. Changes in grade, texture, color, varying viewpoints or vistas are the only guideposts necessary to lead and distinguish space as public or private. Water can divide or bring together the here and there.

The sequence of movement cannot stop at the edge, for edges must be a part of the park; the buildings define the edge enclose other spaces, extending space like the thrusting arches of Chartres.

The scale of the River demands a like response. A bold concept and development of this greatest of spaces with its design resources and psychological value is called for by the very potential of the riverfront. The space can be a satisfying reward of living in the city. Forming a continuous edge, the River could provide orientation, direction, and a strong goal of an alternative environment, connected to East and West City and the Central Business District by a series of paths. The River must be open, easy to reach. More people must have access to the qualities of surface—calming, inviting—and the sounds, the horns, and the ripples.

*Potential of Large-Scale Earth Forms.* Parks may be programmed for functions, like sports events or picnicking, according to the discussion in the introductory brochure. However, parks must be programmed for experience, extent, and sequence. This drawing by architect Michael Southworth was drawn, 12″ × 12″, on vellum with a china marking pencil.

*Riverfront Concept Sketch.* This drawing, also by architect Michael Southworth, was drawn, 6″ × 6″, on vellum with a felt pen. A section of it is shown here, enlarged, as it appeared in the presentation. Dramatic results can be achieved in this manner. The reproduction was in sepia, on a light-screened background just as this is. (Following this drawing in the actual presentation is a dramatic pull-out map of the river front which includes Belle Island and Zug Island in sepia and apple green with the river at the bottom in bright blue.)

Much of the positive qualities of the Inner City are derived from environmental sources. Resources may vary from rooftops to life styles, paving patterns to memorable journeys or vistas. They may be a single building or an entire district. Or they may be a place, a spot where people gather, a point that seems suddenly cooler or warmer, a change in grade, an enclosing space out of the wind or sunny or shady spot. Resources can be places of special activities like college campuses or a corner newsstand or a park or a street where children play.

The concern of this report is that in the inevitable redevelopment of the Inner City these resources are not overlooked and indeed might be positive elements around which to build. There is also the concern that the task of rebuilding be looked upon from an optimistic point of view—not only of all the deficiencies that must be corrected, but also all the physical advantages the Inner City possesses.

It is the hope of this report to stimulate the residents and other users of the Inner City to more carefully consider their immediate environment and what they care about within it. In this way the resource catalogue could grow with contributions from many sources.

Organized facades are apparent in the older, larger buildings such as the Public Library, Harper Hospital, and Cass Technical High School. These facades should be used to terminate vistas, define open space, or act as centers around which the community can build...

*Old Country Building.* On the cover of one of the brochures is this rendering in pencil on vellum drawn by architect Richard Farley. It was drawn to the size of the brochure, 12″ square. This brochure, entitled *Inner City Resources*, is a kind of catalogue of buildings which constitute an important part of the heritage of the city.

*Old Main Building, Wayne University.* This drawing by architect Ronald Margolis was in ink on vellum, 12″ square.

*Bonstelli Theater.* The original of this drawing by architect Alan Melting was only 5″ × 4″. In the brochure it was enlarged to 12″ wide. (Here the enlargement is somewhat less, but it gives some idea of the printed result.)

*Row Houses—Avery Terrace.* Row houses such as these are typical of the way cities like Detroit provided housing in an earlier day. The original drawing was 8″ square and rendered with a ballpoint pen on mimeograph paper by architect Charles Harris. In the brochure, this drawing was produced 12″ square and line work was screened, making it look like a pencil drawing.

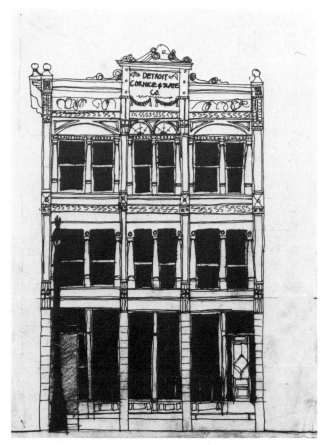

*Detroit Cornice and Slate Company Building.* Architect Ronald Margolis drew this handsome old building in ink and pencil on vellum, 12″ square.

*Street Texture.* In older areas of the city where traffic demands have not replaced the original pavement with concrete, more interesting patterns like this one remain. Where residential redevelopment is anticipated, street textures such as this should be preserved. This drawing in ink and pencil was done by Architect Richard Farley. The original is 4″ × 4″, but in the brochure it was enlarged to 12″ × 12″. Here it is almost in its original size.

Vistas are those openings within the form of the city allowing panoramic or directed views. An example, which should be preserved, is the vista of the Fisher Building along the line of Second Boulevard. The Freeway spaces offer many potential vistas, but unfortunately there is not much to view.

Closure is the terminating of a space such as the closure of the street space at Park Avenue at Peterborough. This quality occurs many times within the Woodward Corridor when intersecting streets do not line up or are discontinuous. This again is a potential to use to advantage and to preserve.

Gateways are those literal or implied entrances to special areas within the City. They can be formed by buildings or spaces. An example is the underpass on North Woodward (a literal gateway) or the opposing Public Library and Art Institute (an implied gateway). The physical form can announce human activities.

*St. Mary's Church.* Typical of the eclectic building and its era is this small-scale European cathedral. The drawing, in pencil on vellum, 12″ square, was by architect Ronald Margolis.

*Trowbridge House.* A more modest residence than the Hecker is this Georgian house. The rendering, in pencil on vellum, 9″ square, is by Ronald Margolis.

*Hecker House.* This magnificent Victorian house is another resource of the Inner City the Plan Commission will preserve. The drawing in ink on vellum is reproduced here, as it was in the brochure, in reverse—that is, white on black—for dramatic emphasis. The drawing, 9″ square, is by architect Ronald Margolis.

*Getaway—First Presbyterian and Church of Christ*. This rendering in pencil on vellum, 12″ square, is by architect Noel Copeland.

*Fisher Building Vista*. The drawing, originally 6″ square, is reproduced 12″ square in the brochure. It is by architect Michael Southworth in pencil on vellum.

*Metropolitan Building*. The early Woodward Plan is responsible not only for the vistas that will be retained in the new plan, but for the closures like this one with the Metropolitan Building as its focal point. This drawing in pencil on vellum is by architect Michael Southworth.

The package of housing ideas is tied to a physical re-development framework alternative for the Inner City. This design framework does not establish the design of individual projects and the design of architecture. It indicates how each individual project may relate to adjacent projects in general architectural form, open space pattern, community facilities and circulation...

This proposal includes substantial rehabilitation of existing sound units and their incorporation into the design of the community of new structures. The new structures are of three types: the rows as in the Redevelopment proposal, medium-rise replacing incompatible uses along Gratiot, and walk-up apartments midblock with free passage beneath. With a substantial amount of rehabilitation, the existing block patterns are more difficult to modify...

The environmental quality of Washington Boulevard would complement a high-quality development, especially since a great diversity of high-quality service functions is available nearby. Because of convenient access routes from all parts of the city, and because the site is large, inexpensive, and 50 percent cleared of any structures, adequate parking will be provided. The excellent exposure of the site will, what is more, make the building a landmark.

Orchestra Place is tied to a physical design framework for the Inner City. Stretching north from the Central Business District is an intricate texture of the Woodward Corridor terminated by the New Center. Many imageable subdistricts are packed into this unique area and the result is an atmosphere of intense activity and life. Woodward Avenue has long been the "main street" of the city and just as in many smaller Midwestern cities and towns, many of the libraries, churches, museums and hospitals line its path. Even a few fine old residences exist, dating from days when "main street" was covered with carriages. Today the Corridor stretches to Pontiac, the trip takes an hour rather than a day, and development of the city has expanded in all directions. But the Inner City segment of the Corridor is still the most diverse and dynamic part, and it provides one of the vital links between the Inner and Outer City . . .

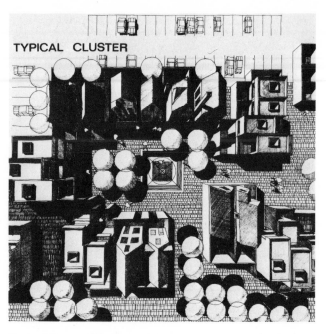

*Typical Cluster*. This integral structure perspective might normally be incomprehensible to the average person, but architect James Velleco "explains" the notion of cluster housing in a way most people would understand. The original in ink and pencil is on vellum, 12" square.

*Redevelopment Housing*. Although designed to be easily understood by the layman, the Detroit study made use of what normally might be considered technical drawings, like these sections of a housing complex. The drawing by architect Alan Melting was in pencil on vellum, 12" × 24".

*Washington Boulevard—Grand River Avenue.* An idea of the complexion of new downtown structures is presaged in this roof plan and drawing by architect Alexander Pollock. Some notion of the radial boulevards is apparent here too. Both drawings are in India ink on vellum.

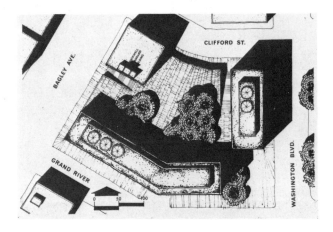

*Orchestra Place.* The cover of the Orchestra Place brochure is an abstract of some of the new combination storage, offices, commerce and housing for the periphery of the district.

*The Building System.* Another integral structure perspective like the previous one by James Velleco. This one is by architect Ronald Margolis and includes existing and new structures, giving the "feel" of the pedestrian character of Orchestra Place.

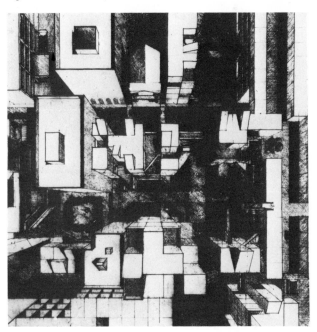

175

The basic purpose of a Cultural Center is to expand the cultural life by opening new horizons—new avenues of cultural, social, economic and educational growth for today and generations hence. In the plan are a Hall of Man, a Planetarium, a Museum of Science and Technology, a Center for the Musical Arts, a Center for the Theater Arts, and the Institute of Arts with people going to the Hall of Man from the art gallery through a magnificent park which would recall the great gardens of the Italian Renaissance; relaxing by a pool while enjoying the sunlit sculpture displayed outdoors; coming from a play or opera on a warm summer night and stopping to enjoy the new and intriguing exhibits at the Planetarium or Hall of Science. It is to serve all age groups from pre-school art exhibits and workshops to well-designed educational facilities for elementary, junior high, senior high, college and postgraduate students, and even beyond to specifically designed facilities for the growing population of retired citizens. It will be a living monument dedicated to the needs of people throughout their life . . .

Intensive residential and induced private educational developments in the immediate vicinity of the Cultural Center will provide in this location one of the most exciting and economically important areas in the region. The Center was conceived and initiated more than 50 years ago with the Art Institute, designed by Paul Phillippe Cret, and the Detroit Public Library by Cass Gilbert. The Detroit Cultural Center entered its greatest phase with the intensive development activity of the past 15 years. Since 1945 Wayne University alone has added more than a dozen buildings, which together with land acquisitions has represented an investment of more than $40,000,000.00. Other developments have included the International Institute, the Rackham Educational Memorial, the new Art School of the Society of Arts and Crafts, the campus of the Merrill-Palmer Institute, and the addition to the Public Library . . .

Architect Kenneth Neuman is responsible for this drawing of a proposed Natural History Museum. It was in pencil on vellum, 9" square.

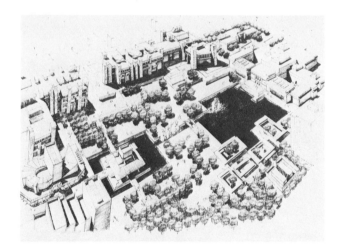

*Cultural Center Perspective/1900.* It is fitting to end this presentation of Detroit/1990 with this fine bird's-eye view of the cultural center by architect Alan Melting. The original in pencil on vellum was 23" × 34".

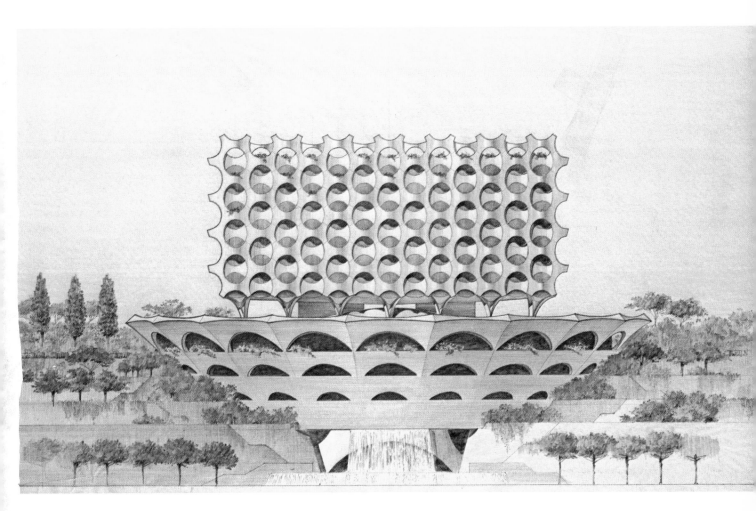

**Renderer:** Joseph Salerno
**Architect:** Joseph Salerno
*Proposed hotel* 1957, Rome, Italy

On yellow tracing paper, 18″ × 22½″, this rendering is in graphite pencil and three colored pencils: green, ochre, and burnt sienna. Mr. Salerno says that his philosophy of presentation is to provide the maximum of information with the minimum of fuss. A rendering of this kind is useful only for display and for presentation to the client. It is virtually impossible to reproduce the drawing in black and white because of the extreme delicacy of the lines.

**Renderer:** Gino Misciagna
**Interior Designers:** Griswold, Heckel and Kelly

**New York Telephone Company Offices** New York, N.Y.

A very important part of any interiors presentation is color. Most interior designers or architects who handle their own interiors use samples of floor or ceiling tile, wood paneling, carpeting, fabrics, plants, and other objects. In this way the client can see exactly what is being proposed. Nevertheless, some designers want color renderings that exactly match the sample colors.

In Gino Misciagna's drawing of the New York Telephone Company's conference room, exact color match was essential, but his use of Zippatone toning is also of more than passing interest. In the mirror wall at left he was able to produce two tones of gray with one Zippatone gray tone sheet. This is particularly apparent in the vertical and diagonal lines: some are very dark while others are quite light. This effect, which is achieved by laying the tone on the drawing but not pressing the Zippatone down evenly, is not discernible even on the actual drawing. (See the ink-line base drawing of this rendering on p. 76).

**Renderer:** Herbert J. Gute
**Architect:** Carlin & Pozzi

**Redevelopment Project** New Haven Development Corporation

Herbert Gute is primarily a watercolor painter whose work hangs in numerous permanent collections. It is natural, then, that he start his rendering with a light, cool watercolor wash. This establishes the value pattern, which is essential. The rendering is executed on watercolor paper over a pencil perspective. Mr. Gute generally puts in the background first and then relates the building to it, but sometimes he works the other way. He has devised his own acrylic medium made up of watercolors, gouache, and dry pigments.

**Renderer:** Norman Jaffe
**Architect:** Norman Jaffe
**Three Houses on Shelter Island** Off the North
Shore of Long Island in New York State

The original color rendering of these three houses
(reproduced in black and white on page 30) was
executed on full-sheet watercolor paper, 22″ × 38″.
In the illustration, the Seidler house is at left, the
Osofsky house is in the center, and the Jacobs
house is at right.

**Renderer:** Barry Zauss
**Architects:** Gruen Associates
**Linear Village and Pedestrian Tunnel** Snowmass
at Aspen, Aspen, Colorado

The original of this rendering was executed in ink on illustration board, 16″ × 26″. Like most of the Gruen firm's presentations, this was then made into a color slide.

Snowmass consists of 3,500 acres with a master plan that ultimately will comprise three villages. Gruen Associates are in the process of further developing the first of these, the West Village. The site is across the ski slope, where the terrain is on a 20 percent slope. The expansion will follow the contour of the hillside until it reaches the eastern ski slope. The new development will be organized along the pedestrian spine and connect to the existing commercial center at West Village by means of a tunnel under the ski slope. The mall will extend 1,800 feet to the eastern ski slope. The western end contains 70 percent of the commercial area and will be enclosed with a glass roof. It will have shopping and restaurants as well as lodges and condominiums. The tunnel also will contain a number of small boutiques and specialty shops. The focal point of the mall is a large nightclub and a penny arcade that will be treated as a casino pit.

**Renderer:** James Morrison Leefe
**Architects and Engineers:** Giffels Associates, Inc.
**General Electric Research and Development Center** Twinsburg, Ohio

James Leefe uses Zippatone and pantone for color accents, which makes it possible for others to pitch in at the last-minute presentation rush. For all the details of this project, see pages 153–154.

# 10. COMPUTER PERSPECTIVE

Many architects fear that the computer, used to produce perspectives, will somehow interfere with the creativity of the designer. This is conceivable, of course, but about as likely as the possibility of an outside renderer interfering with the design process. A renderer, given incomplete information on some detail, could, conceivably, fill it in to suit himself and, perhaps, in the end find he had actually designed it.*

Innovative architects have been intrigued by the computer for years and, as a result, some large offices have installations of their own. Small and medium-sized firms can utilize the computer through outside service bureaus. Few, if any, independent renderers would find computer perspectives as economical as hand-drawn ones. However, in an architectural office the computer has many uses.

One of these is estimating. The computer can examine different design solutions simply and accurately. A good architectural program would be designed to produce architectural graphics, graphic standards, and time studies of construction processes—in short, a quantity survey. Such a program would call forth concrete, reinforcing rods, steel, aluminum or wood framing, wall paneling, flooring, elevator cabs, shafts, and all other materials and equipment that go into a building.

A program like this, once designed and coded, can be used repeatedly with slightly different input to suit local conditions. The output can print out, in logical sequence, from grading and formwork to such minor finish details as moldings and plates for electrical switches and outlets. Quantities of materials and hours of labor multiplied by current costs would make comparative cost estimates among schemes quick and easy. CPM (Critical Path Method) charts coded into the memory will assure that when construction is under way, components will be delivered in the correct order for fabrication.

This book is not the place to present a beginner's course in computers—there are numerous text-

*The late Hugh Ferriss was official renderer for the original United Nations tower in New York. A great controversy arose during the early design stages between the architects from the U.S.S.R., who wanted the building "planted firmly in the ground," and the representatives of France and Brazil, Le Corbusier and Oscar Niemeyer, who wanted it to "float." Mr. Ferriss told the author that, as renderer, he solved the problem by filling in the space between the ground and the second story with entourage, thus not merely avoiding an international incident but, perhaps, saving the UN from its first *"nyet."*

books that do just that. Nevertheless, everyone should know that a computer system consists roughly of hardware and software and that computer hardware is generally thought of as being of three types: input devices, central processing units (CPU), and output devices. Output devices of particular interest to the architects are the various computer-controlled drawing machines. The CPU is directly connected to the motors and pen of a machine upon which a piece of paper is mounted. Circuits within the CPU are activated by the operating program to drive the motors which move the pen to different positions on the paper. If the pen is held down on the paper while it is being moved, a line is drawn.

If someone buys or rents a computer, he should get a CPU, some assortment of input/output devices and an operating system. If the user is not rich, he can buy or rent a computer terminal, which frequently has a cathode ray tube or other electronic display, and then buy a telephone hook-up service and computer operating time on a remote computer. (Terminals are connected to CPUs by long wires and may even be connected by acoustic couplers, which transmit and receive special audio signals via ordinary telephone lines.)

When the computing system is intended to be used by architects who are not computer specialists, part of the operating system is a special (and very valuable) program called a compiler or an interpreter. The compiler will convert application programs, which are written in languages that are somewhat easy for people to understand, into the switch settings and circuit operations which will activate the CPU. The language a compiler translates into machine instructions is what must be learned to program the computer. Of course the better an individual learns the languages and the more he understands the nature of the computer itself, the better he can program, but, in general, the minimum knowledge required is at least one compiler language—termed a high-level computer language—and a few job control commands. These job control commands are necessary to tell the operating system what language the user is using and what input/output devices or other computer facilities, such as a plotter, the program will use.

Except that a plotter and a graphic display system are required to draw lines, the production of drawings of any type by computer is, actually easier than the production of estimates and specifications. Since architects are primarily concerned with drawing, it is only natural that their first interest in computer graphics would have developed early on. The first conference on computer graphics in architecture was held in Boston in 1964 and Yale was host to a similar conference in 1968. Nicholas Negroponte of M.I.T. and Eric Teicholz of Harvard, among others, are pioneers in the field. The four years between the Boston and New Haven Conferences were years of dramatic change in the state of the art.

Today, computer graphics is a broad field primarily concerned with all aspects of software and hardware that involve people communicating with computers via pictures. The elementary problem of computer graphics is the programming of the plotting devices. That is, how easily to control the motors, the cathode-ray tube displays, the movie-generating equipment that will draw lines, curves, lettering, colors, and changes in the picture. The motors of a plotter are usually designed to move a small angle every time they receive short-duration voltage signals. These signals cannot be generated by the CPU too fast or the motor will not respond; also the CPU must keep account of how many signals are given to the motors to insure that the pen moves in the path desired. Clever programs are required for this—programs hopefully so easy to use that the nonspecialist programmer need not concern himself with the details of the plotting device. A more complicated problem is the development of techniques by which a user can draw upon a cathode-ray tube. It may appear to an observer that the user of a cathode-ray tube is writing on the display. The actual sequence of events is somewhat more involved. The instrument used to draw with is a light pen. It looks like a thick ball-point pen but actually is a photoresistor or a photocell. What the light pen does is to detect light. On the screen something must be drawn initially by the computer, and the user points to parts of the illuminated picture. The machine can detect what parts of the picture are pointed to, and, in accordance with the procedure specified by the computer program, the picture will change. Imagine a picture of a floor plan. If some features of the floor plan are to be deleted and if the program controlling the display is expecting to delete features, all the user need do is point the light pen at those features to be deleted and they will disappear. To add features, one must use a cursor, which is a moving spot or any more complicated symbol that will follow the light pen. The user can position the cursor and then by varied means clue the computer as to the type of feature to draw where the cursor is. The clueing techniques are up to the program designer and a common procedure is to point first to a selection of features at the side or bottom of the screen and then move the cursor.

Some of the more elegant problems of computer graphics do not involve the picture directly but are concerned with the description of the objects contained in it. For example, if a description of a building is read into the computer, and if a realistic picture of the building is desired from any viewpoint, the appearance of the building can be calculated. All the lines or edges of the building can be drawn, or hidden features can be suppressed, or the shadows cast at varied times of the day can be drawn. What makes these problems difficult is that the machine cannot specifically see the picture as a draftsman does, so mathematical techniques must be invented so that the blind machine by calculation can detect where lines cross, where light rays pierce surfaces, and other problems handled instinctively by the very human draftsman.

The use of computers is increasing for several reasons. Obviously, in some applications, considerable savings in time and money are realized. Some operations of our increasingly complex society would now be impossible without automatic information processing. The operation of oil refineries, the credit card economy, aerospace adventures, the design of large buildings are thoroughly dependent on computers. Perhaps the major reason for computer proliferation is the missionary zeal of the computer community. Originally, the programming of computers was a very difficult task, and early programmers needed to have talents in mathematics, logic, electronics, and also such personality traits as imagination, tenacity, patience,

concentration, and a bit of ESP. Fortunately, a great many people have worked very hard to make it possible for more ordinary persons to program and use computers. While some aptitude is still required, it has been well demonstrated that the average technically trained individual can proram his own problems. To those who are not computer buffs, the future is almost scary since both the price and complexity of the computer hardware and software are decreasing. It thus behooves even those frightened by the computer to keep a sharp eye and ear on the scene. Sophisticated programs require a large expensive computer, so means have been devised to share computer capability, as previously indicated. The architect-user with his small remote graphic display system and plotter eventually will tie into a larger remote system. It will not be long before even independent renderers can afford computer perspectives, though at present the cost would be too high. For a preview of the machines that will make this possible, the excellent Hewlett-Packard electronic desk calculator should be examined. Originally available for a mere $5000, its price recently was reduced to $395 from $495. It is likely that within a few years calculators like this may be available for as little as $25. And means to make them capable of producing print-outs and for tying into consoles and plotters will be available for slightly more. At present it is a little difficult to arrive at the big, one-time cost of an architectural program. It is time-consuming—that is what makes it expensive. That is why architects who have developed programs guard them zealously. The IBM 1130, which is required for an architectural program, rents for $1000 per month, but this cost is likely to come down. The cathode-ray tube, which displays the output as on a TV screen, also rents for $1000 per month and will probably continue to cost that much. A plotter is a one-time cost and can be bought outright for about $1000. This price is not likely to come down either. And since all architectural programs are similar, it is likely that ultimately those who have developed multi-purpose programs will rent out their capability to help cover their original cost. So it is clear that small and medium-sized architectural firms will soon be able to afford a computer.

## DEVELOPING A SIMPLE PROGRAM

How to make a computer produce lines of lengths and directions desired for a perspective is best explained by taking a simple example and writing a program for it. The prerequisite mathematics have been left out in order to be able to concentrate only on the steps necessary to provide the computer with material essential to drive it to produce a perspective.

Consider the problem of producing a perspective drawing via the medium of a computer-controlled peripheral device, a plotter; normally when writing a program for a computer, it is first necessary to understand the overall (global) plan for the program and thereafter shape it until it is in a useful form by fleshing in the details. Let us follow this general approach here.

The basic idea is to find a suitable representation for the object to be drawn as seen from the desired perspective point. Let us imagine the object is as shown here—a block of offices.

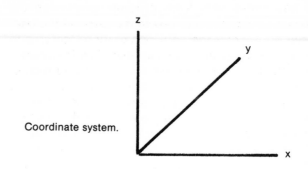

Coordinate system.

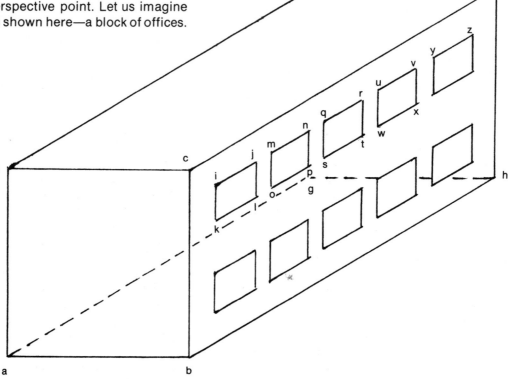

Let us also assume that we are interested only in a line drawing without the hidden lines removed; removal of these lines can be attended to in more sophisticated programs. In this case we can represent the object or model as a set of corners or nodes connected by straight lines.

This representation dominates the rest of the program, and the choice or its raison d'etre never explicitly appears thereafter in the program but is crucial in terms of understanding how the program works, its results, and the sequence of instructions necessary to produce it.

This simple drawing may now be represented by the following recipe or program flow:

Point 'a' with coordinates $(x_1y_1z_1)$ with respect to a given coordinate system is connected by a straight line to point 'b' which has coordinates $(x_2y_2z_2)$ with respect to the same coordinate system. Similarly, point 'b' with coordinates $(x_2y_2z_2)$ is connected to 'c' with coordinates $(x_3y_3z_3)$, and so on.

If we now write $(x_1y_1z_1)$ to represent point 'a' and the symbol $\longrightarrow$ to represent "is connected to 'b' by a straight line," then the program flow for the drawing above can be written as:

$a\ (x_1y_1z_1) \longrightarrow b\ (x_2y_2z_2)$

$b\ (x_2y_2z_2) \longrightarrow c\ (x_3y_3z_3)$

$c\ (x_3y_3z_3) \longrightarrow d\ (x_4y_4z_4)$

$d\ (x_4y_4z_4) \longrightarrow a\ (x_1y_1z_1)$

$a\ (x_1y_1z_1) \longrightarrow g\ (x_5y_5z_5)$

$g\ (x_5y_5z_5) \longrightarrow e\ (x_7y_7z_7)$

$e\ (x_7y_7z_7) \longrightarrow f\ (x_8y_8z_8)$

$f\ (x_8y_8z_8) - \rightarrow g\ (x_5y_5z_5)$

$g\ (x_5y_5z_5) \longrightarrow h\ (x_6y_6z_6)$    (note: redrawn)

$h\ (x_6y_6z_6) \longrightarrow b\ (x_2y_2z_2)$

$b\ (x_2y_2z_2) \longrightarrow c\ (x_3y_3z_3)$    (note: redrawn)

$c \qquad \longrightarrow e$ etc.

$e \qquad \longrightarrow f$    (note: redrawn)

$f \qquad \longrightarrow d$

And this can be taken to be the program to generate the figure with $a \longrightarrow b$ as the first instruction, $b \longrightarrow c$ the second, and so forth.

We notice that as we have specified this sequence, we have not lifted our pen and will have redrawn at least three lines. Other ordering schemes for drawing the same figure with eight corners might necessitate redrawing more than three lines. If we allow pen lifting, we could order the machine to avoid redrawing. Furthermore, this scheme is not restricted to producing, for example, merely regular geometrical figures. Any figure defined by a set of eight points in space will do. Note also that the coordinate that appears on the right-hand column also appears on the left side of the next line. This raises an important point. If we interpret the mnemonic $a \longrightarrow b$ to imply the drafting *procedure:* pen up (i.e., don't draw) go to position a, pen down to to b and stop, then the preceding list need not be followed in sequence and each instruction can be executed unilaterally. If, on the other hand, we allow ourselves to be constrained to plot in a specified order, then we may drop the right-hand side and merely give the list of coordinates in sequence—a, b, c, d, a, g, h, e, f, g, h, b, c, e, f, d, with the understanding: go from a to b, next go from b to c, next go from c to d, next go from d to a, etc., that is move incrementally from where you are to where you want to be.

Now if we wished to draw a figure with an arbitrary number of vertices, we can do so in both of these representations merely by adding new points to the sequence and specifying which should be connected to which and in what order.

If we allow ourselves to be constrained further only to cubical or 8-pointed figures, we need only specify two of the faces, say a, b, c, d and g, h, e, f, and we can arrange (i.e., write another program) so that the computer will copy the appropriate vertices to produce the desired list:

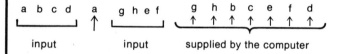

Fig. 1

Now we have supplied much less information to the machine (only 8 vertices) but, *caveat emptor*, if the vertices are supplied in the wrong order—say a, b, c, d   h, e, f, g—a distorted picture will result. This will *not* be a computer error but will be caused by faulty input data.

The computer here will assume that the desired figure is represented by the list:

Fig. 2

where Figure 2 is obtained from Figure 1 by code substitution of h, e, f, g, for g, h, e, f. This would result in the drawing:

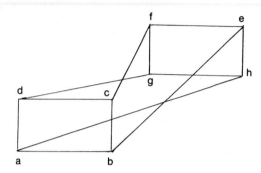

in which a twist is evident, since we permuted the order of drawing the side g, h, e, f. Note also that the model here has been specified in absolute coordinates. An incremental recipe could also have been used, for example, up 3 feet—along 2 feet, and so on.

To draw the windows of the building, the same procedure is followed, but now we only need 4 points per window. If the windows are identical, we can copy the window with a new starting point and use of an incremental definition.

Now that we generally understand the problem—the representation and the plan—we can begin to think about how to implement the drawing. At the first level, we need some results in analytic geometry and then, on the second, we need to know how to draw a line.

First, the analytic geometry. We have decomposed the drawing of the complicated structure shown at the beginning to the problem of a studied repetition of the basic operation of drawing a straight line in space between two points, say a $(x_1y_1z_1)$ and b $(x_2y_2z_2)$.

Since we are drawing on a two-dimensional sheet, we need a projection point 'p,' a projection plane 'P,' a distance 'f,' the focal length between them. As is well known, a straight line in space projects either into a straight line or a point which is a degenerate straight line. It is possible to find a formula in a mathematics book which gives the coordinates of the image of point 'a' in the projection plane 'P,' say $a^1(x_p y_p)$. Similarly, we can find the co-ordinates of $b^1(x_p y_p)$.

The accompanying drawing from the *Scientific American* shows that it is not necessary in projecting a perspective by computer to reverse the image. The computer, once it is fed the proper information, can provide innumerable views of the object. The Ueland and Junker drawings and those from the Pennsylvania State University later in this chapter are evidence of the possibilities.

The straight line joining 'a' to 'b' in the real model will give a straight line joining $a^1$ to $b^1$ in the projection plane. Thus, the next major step in our program is to apply the projection formula to all the points in our input list or sequence in order to find the points to be drawn in the desired picture. Let us assume this is done.

Only now do we have to consider the actual plotting of points or drawing of lines. This depends on the characteristics of the plotter used. Sometimes the hardware requires a starting point, and a direction or vector to go in and a distance to go, sometimes it requires the starting coordinates and the final coordinates, and sometimes all it requires is the final coordinate and assumes that it will start from its present position. In any case this is a technical detail and is specified in the manual describing the device.

Putting together the sequence list, the little piece of analytic geometry, and the program to draw a straight line, will allow any perspective view of a wire model in three-dimensional space to be drawn. This general capability of generating multiple views from different vantage points is of course bought at the price of detailed specification of the model and discipline in writing the program.

The philosophy in summary is: Understand the representation of the problem, break it down into the smallest understandable piece—here a straight line joining two points—and then rebuild, using this concept. The points a user must look out for lie in the implicit constraints in the program and in failing to recognize them.

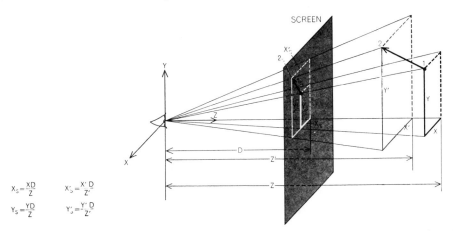

$$X_s = \frac{XD}{Z} \qquad X'_s = \frac{X'D}{Z'}$$

$$Y_s = \frac{YD}{Z} \qquad Y'_s = \frac{Y'D}{Z'}$$

Perspective projection for a computer display is obtained by placing the original of the coordinate system at the observer's eye. The projection of all points on the screen is then readily computed from the geometry of similar triangles. The diagram shows how the two end points, 1 and 2, of an arrow are projected to the points $1_s$ and $2_s$. The first equation states that $x_s$ is to x as the distance to the screen, D, is to z. Other dimensions are obtained similarly. (Diagram and caption from "Computer Display" by Ivan E. Sutherland. Copyright © June 1970 by Scientific American, Inc. All rights reserved.)

## ARCHITECTURE AND COMPUTERS

Just how precisely a computer can plot a perspective is evident in the accompanying series of drawings from the offices of Ueland and Junker, Architects, of Philadelphia. According to Mark Ueland, a computer service wanted to show what it could do and helped the architects with the expensive programming. After that, views of the project could be turned out by the hundreds in a matter of minutes. There is no need to go into the intricacies here but the sample, herewith, illustrates the kind of input that is necessary for a fisheye perspective like that shown in some of the perspectives designed by Gunnar Birkerts at the end of this chapter.

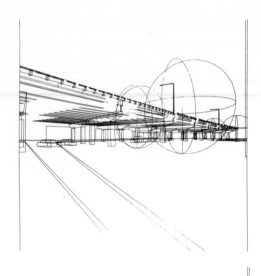

The drawings are of the Delaware Expressway Air Rights Study. The first three are general views, while the next two are more detailed. They consist of a base line drawing of the highway produced by Satellite Computer Corporation which has been overlaid with handmade drawings of the architect's design proposal. The base drawings were produced by an electronic plotter in about fifteen minutes, each from a computer program created from input provided by the architect to the programmer. This consisted of plans and sections of the portions of the highway to be represented. The last drawing is another rendering—this one an aerial view of a proposed recreation building—prepared from the computer output. These base drawings were done at the beginning of the study and served as aids to design development. One feature of the computer drawing technique that was not utilized by the architects is the capability of producing views of the same object from all possible points of view with only minor changes in the program which had been prepared previously.

The architects found the computer drawing technique to be neither significantly more or less expensive than constructing equivalent drawings by hand in the office. What interested the architects most about the process was the pictorial quality of the drawings produced, especially their precise detail and their illusion of transparency.

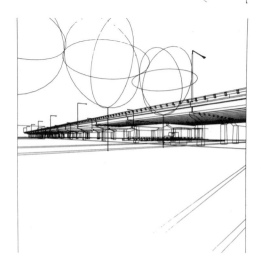

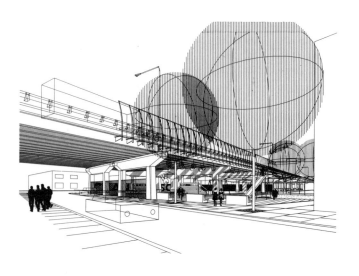

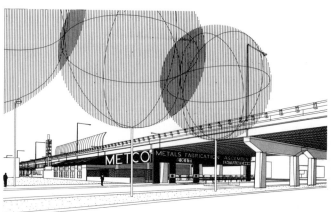

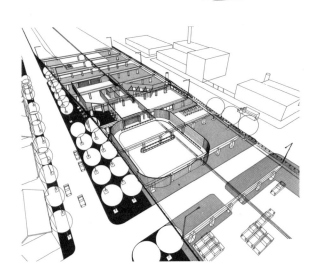

Arthur Appel of the IBM Research Center in Yorktown Heights, New York, is a specialist in computer graphics. He has developed a program that can calculate architectural perspectives as well as perspectives of aircraft, machines, machine parts, the human head, and nearly any object he would care to call forth. His papers include such esoterica as "The Visibility Problem in Machine Rendering of Solids"; "The Notion of Quantitative Invisibility and the Machine Rendering of Solids"; "Shadows without Substance: Some Techniques for Shading Machine Renderings of Solids"; and "Interactive Graphics in Data Processing: Modeling in Three Dimensions." Having mastered the art of turning out perspectives with and without hidden lines, he developed programs to produce perspectives with shading. A project that he undertook with the programming assistance of Arthur Stein was recorded in a paper entitled "Computer Generated Development of Polyhedra." In it the authors describe how a computer can design patterns to be folded into three-dimensional shapes. The same data used to make paper or cardboard models. Mr. Appel has also worked with Dr. R. Pole to produce slides to be used with a special glass, which, though only 4″ × 5″, consists of 2000 fly's-eye lenses. With the lens it is possible to view these slides, called holocodings, and when the viewer moves his eye around, the object changes as if it were seen in three dimensions from innumerable viewpoints. These holocodings are ordinary light holograms and are somewhat like windows into an imaginary space.

Professor Ray Masters of the Department of Architecture at Pennsylvania State University has provided two series of perspectives developed from his Bix Blox program. The first series, of the Chamber's Building on the university campus, are conventional perspective views moving in toward the building. The second set is a complex experimental project slated to provide housing and office space, designed by Gunnar Birkerts and Associates under a grant from the Graham Foundation. Before the drawings, a sample of the input required for the project is shown. The BLOCKS package describes the LOOKS package and specifies the number and type of perspectives. Included in this selection from the series of computer-driven drawings are

some fisheye perspectives, straight plans and elevations, and conventional perspectives which display the amazing range of views available once the program is set up. Views from any conceivable angle and truncated views such as are shown here can be turned out in a matter of minutes.

Things are developing fast in the field of computer graphics. The Bibliography includes references to important work in the area for readers interested in delving into the matter and following developments in the field.

A walk through Chambers Building.

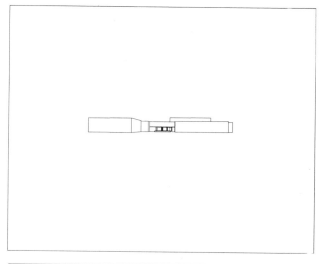

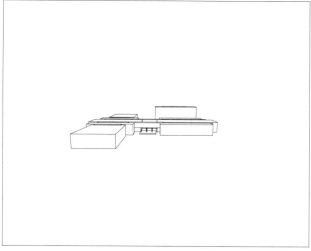

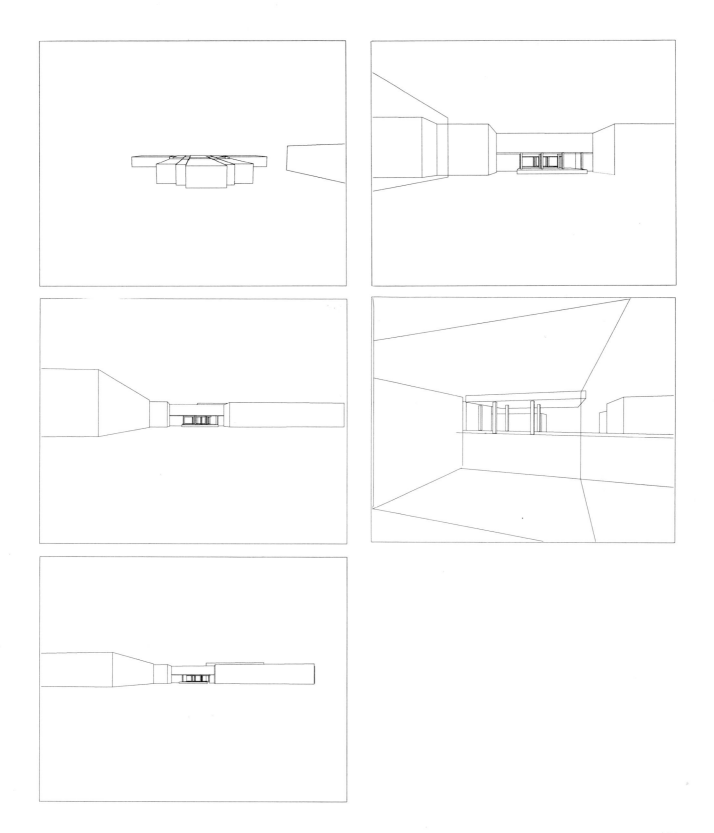

Sample input for Gunnar Birkerts project.

```
// EXEC PGM=BIGBLOX
//STEPLIB DD DSN=SYS1.AFLIB,UNIT=2314,VOL=SER=MODCON,DISP=SHR
//FT06F001 DD SYSOUT=A
//FT07F001 DD UNIT=2400-1,VOL=SER=LEEGEO,DISP=OLD,LABEL=(1,NL),
// DCB=(RECFM=FB,LRECL=80,BLKSIZE=1600,DEN=1,TRTCH=ET)
//FT05F001 DD *
SIZE
  .10
BLOCKS    P
     0    0   16   14   24   20
     4   24    0    6    6   58
    10   20    6   24   14   10
     0   30   16   14   24   20
    10   20   36   24   14   20
    34   24    0    6    6   58
    40   20    6   24   14   30
    64   24    0    6    6   38
    70   20    6   24   14   10
    94   24    0    6    6   38
     4   54    0    6    6   38
     0   60   16   14   24   10
    64   54    0    6    6   58
     2   84    0    6    6   58
    10   80   36   24   14   20
    34   84    0    6    6   58
    40   80   36   24   14   20
    40   80    6   24   14   10
    64   84    0    6    6   58
     0   90   16   14   24   20
     4  114    0    6    6   38
    64  114    0    6    6   38
    70  110    6   24   14   10
    94  114    0    6    6   18
     0  120   16   14   24   20
     4  144    0    6    6   58
    10  140    6   24   14   10
    10  140   36   24   14   20
    34  144    0    6    6   58
    40  140   16   24   14   30
    64  144    0    6    6   58
    70  140   36   24   14   20
    94  144    0    6    6   58
99999
LOOKS
    3
VIEW NUMBER ONE
    -11.0      7.5      2.5       0     7.5    3.0   11  8.5  4.0      1
VIEW NUMBER TWO
     28.0      7.5      2.5      10     7.5    2    11  8.5  4.0      1
VIEW NUMBER THREE
     32.0      7.5      3.5      10     7.5    4    11  8.5  6.0      1
END
```

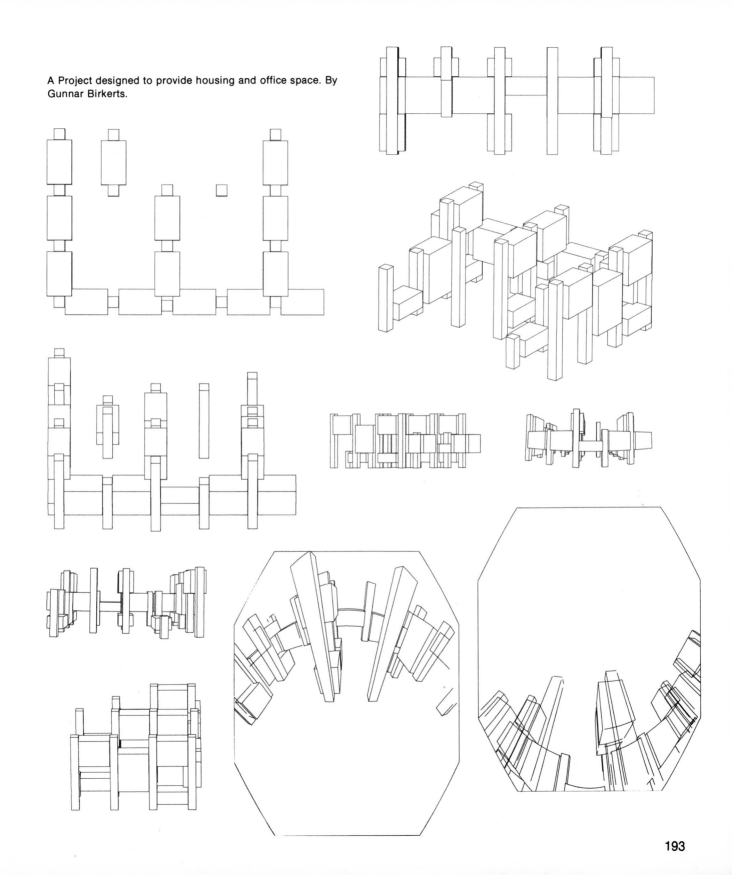

A Project designed to provide housing and office space. By Gunnar Birkerts.

# BIBLIOGRAPHY

## BOOKS

Atkin, William Wilson; Corbelletti, Raniero; and Fiore, Vincent R. *Pencil Techniques in Modern Design*. New York: Reinhold Publishing Corporation, 1953.

Cole, Rex V., *The Artistic Anatomy of Trees*. New York: Dover, 1951.

DePostels, Theodore A. *Fundamentals of Perspective*. New York: Reinhold Publishing Corporation, 1942.

Doblin, Jay. *Perspective: a New System for Designers*. New York: Whitney Library of Design, 1956.

Frees, Ernest Irving. *Perspective Projection*. New York: The Pencil Points Press, Inc., 1930.

Gettens, Rutherford J., and Stout, George L. Introduction by Edward W. Fields. *Painting Materials, a Short Encyclopedia*. New York: D. Van Nostrand, 1942.

Gibson, James J., *Perception of the Visual World*. Boston: Houghton Mifflin Co., 1966.

Guptill, Arthur L. *Pencil Drawing Step by Step, Second Edition*. New York: Reinhold Publishing Corporation, 1959.

Hohauser, Sanford. *Architectural and Interior Models: Design and Construction*. New York: Van Nostrand Reinhold Company, 1970.

Lockard, William Kirby, *Drawing as a Means to Architecture*. New York: Reinhold Book Corporation, 1968.

Mayer, Ralph. *The Artist's Handbook of Materials and Techniques*, Third Edition. New York: The Viking Press, 1970.

Meder, Joseph *Die Handzeichung: Ihre Technik und Entwicklung*. Vienna: Anton Schroll and Co., 1923.

Moskovitz, Ira, selector and editor. *Great Drawings of All Time, French—Thirteenth Century to 1919*, Vol. III. New York: Shorewood Publishers, Inc., 1962.

Saylor, Henry S. *Dictionary of Architecture*. New York: John Wiley & Sons, 1952.

Shulman, Julius. *Photographing Architecture and Interiors*. New York: Whitney Library of Design, 1960.

Whittick, Arnold. *Eric Mendelsohn*. London: Faber & Faber Limited, 1940.

## BROCHURES

DePostels, Theodore A. *The Perspector, Device for Making Perspectives, Angular and Parallel, of Exterior and Interior Views*. New York: Reinhold Publishing Corporation, 1952.

Fleming, Clarence C., and Guptill, Arthur L. *The Pencil, Its History, Manufacture and Use*. Bloomsbury, N.J.: Koh-I-Noor Pencil Co., Inc. 1936.

# INDEX

## Index of Architects' and Designers' Work